The Bagnios of Algiers AND The Gre... ....

The Bagnios of Algiers AND The Great Sultana

TWO PLAYS OF CAPTIVITY

Miguel de Cervantes

EDITED AND TRANSLATED BY

Barbara Fuchs and Aaron J. Ilika

PENN

University of Pennsylvania Press

Philadelphia

Published by

University of Pennsylvania Press

Philadelphia, Pennsylvania 19104-4112

Printed in the United States of America on acid-free paper

10 9 8 7 6 5 4 3 2 1

Library of Congress Cataloging-in-Publication Data

Cervantes Saavedra, Miguel de, 1547-1616.

[Baños de Argel. English]

The bagnios of Algiers; and, The great Sultana: two plays of captivity / Miguel de Cervantes; edited and translated by Barbara Fuchs and Aaron Ilika.

p. cm.

Includes bibliographical references.

ISBN 978-0-8122-4209-6 (alk. paper)

1. Algiers (Algeria)—Drama.   2. Istanbul (Turkey)—Drama.   3. Islam—Drama.   4. Captivity—Drama. 5. Cervantes Saavedra, Miguel de, 1547–1616—Translations into English.   I. Fuchs, Barbara.   II. Ilika, Aaron. III. Cervantes Saavedra, Miguel de, 1547–1616. Gran sultana. English.   IV. Title.

PQ6329.A7F83 2009

862'.3—dc22   2009024357

Para Nicolás, Tomás y Matías, ávidos lectores

Per a l'Anna

Contents

Cervantes, Playwright

Universally renowned as the author of *Don Quixote*, Miguel de Cervantes Saavedra (1547–1616) also wrote multiple plays. He was eager to prove himself as a playwright and poet, since these were the most established measures of literary worth in his time. Cervantes had some early successes on the Madrid stage in the 1580s, yet his later plays never found an audience. He was less facile in the style of the new *comedia*, and the complexity and interest of his prose are somewhat flattened in his verse drama. In 1615, shortly before his death, he chose to publish a collection of his new plays, *Ocho comedias y ocho entremeses nuevos, nunca representados* (Eight New Plays and Interludes, Never Performed). This highly unusual venture, in a period where plays were generally published only after having been exhaustively performed, served Cervantes as an alternative to the theatrical success that eluded him.

Cervantes lived through great transformations in European drama. In the Spanish context, he spans the transition between the early, simple theater of Juan del Encina (1469–1529) and Lope de Rueda (1505?–1565), who wrote religious, comic, and pastoral plays, or eclogues, and the more sophisticated productions of the *comedia nueva*, or new drama, whose most prolific and talented exponent was Félix Lope de Vega Carpio (1562–1635). Had Cervantes's later plays been performed, they would have been staged in a sophisticated, urban, open-air, public theater—the *corral*—where audiences of all classes and of both genders mingled. Successful playwrights sold their work to *autores*, company managers who were a combination of producers and directors. The plays were performed by companies of professional actors of both genders. Hundreds of *comedias* were produced annually to satisfy the audience's seemingly infinite demand for them. The plays were introduced by music and racy dances, with farcical interludes (*entremeses*) performed between the acts.

The prologue to Cervantes's 1615 collection, which includes the two plays translated in our volume, offers a wealth of information on the development of Spanish drama in the period and Cervantes's perception of his place within that literary culture. The author describes a conversation with friends on the state of the theater in Spain. As the oldest interlocutor, Cervantes charts the recent history of the stage based on his own recollections. Lope de Rueda, he explains, "was the first to bring Spanish plays out of the nursery, to exalt them and make of them something to admire" (Cervantes 1995, 23). In that more innocent era, "plays were dialogues, much like eclogues, between two or three shepherds and a shepherdess, enlivened and spaced out by two or three interludes, on either a black woman, a villain, a fool, or a Biscayan" (Cervantes 1995, 24). Moreover, the material trappings of the theater were then as simple as the plays themselves:

> In the time of this famous Spaniard, all the appurtenances of the company's manager fit in one sack, as they were no more than four white shepherd's jackets embossed with gilt leather, four beards, wigs, and shepherd's crooks, and little else. . . . There were no stage machines, nor fights between Moors and Christians, on foot or on horseback; no figure appeared or seemed to appear from the center of the earth through the space beneath the stage, which was made of four benches arranged in a square with four or six planks on top, so that it was raised about four handspans from the floor; nor were there clouds full of angels or souls that descended from the heavens. The theater was adorned with an old blanket, pulled from one side to the other with two strings, to make the tiring room. Behind it were the musicians, singing some old ballad with no guitar to accompany them. (Cervantes 1995, 24)

Gradually, the theater began to acquire some of the accouterments that were missing in the early days. A certain Navarro, Cervantes tells us,

> made plays somewhat more elaborate, moving the costumes to chests and trunks; he moved the music out from behind the blanket, where it had been sung before, onto the stage; he removed

the actors' beards, for until then no-one had acted without a false one, and made them all play their parts barefaced, except for those who were to play old men or other characters who required a change in appearance; he invented machines, clouds, thunder and lightning, challenges and battles, yet none of this reached the lofty pinnacle it occupies today. (Cervantes 1995, 25)

The irony in Cervantes's tone as he ends his description betrays his chagrin, for he has not climbed that lofty pinnacle. Instead, his theatrical production is located at that earlier, intermediate point, when, he tells us, "the theaters of Madrid showed *The Traffic of Algiers*, which I composed, *The Destruction of Numancia*, and *The Naval Battle*." The last of these three has been lost, and the two extant plays do not support Cervantes's claim that he was the first to modernize Spanish drama by reducing five acts to three at this time: both *Traffic* and *Numancia* feature four acts and are written in a ponderous, occasionally allegorical style. Nor can we know whether he in fact wrote "twenty or thirty plays at this time, all of which were performed without meriting an offering of cucumbers or other projectiles" (Cervantes 1995, 25–26). The more likely number is somewhere between ten and twenty, including the eight plays Cervantes published much later, some of which may have been reworked from earlier versions.

According to Cervantes's own narrative, his budding theatrical career was cut short by his attention to other matters and the spectacular arrival of Lope on the scene: "Then came that prodigy of nature, the great Lope de Vega, and stole the crown of playwriting; he overwhelmed all actors and placed them under his rule; he filled the world with his own pleasing and well-made plays—so many, in fact, that he's written over ten thousand pages, and, most remarkably, has seen them all performed" (Cervantes 1995, 26). Lope's success with a new, more nimble theater, which happily abandoned Aristotelian precepts and concerned itself primarily with the great crowd-pleasing themes of honor, marriage, class conflict, and monarchical politics, rendered Cervantes's production old-fashioned and undesirable. In a deeply humiliating exchange that Cervantes nonetheless shares with his readers, a bookseller tells him that, while his prose is well regarded, his verse is not worth much, according to a noted company manager. Piqued, Cervantes turns to his old plays and interludes and decides they are not all bad. He sells them to the self-same bookseller, who publishes them despite the cavils of stage folk. And thus we have the very collection whose prologue the author uses to right matters, or at least to give us his version of events.

Yet despite Cervantes's own bitter assessment of his limited success, there is much to recover in his writings for the theater, some of which incorporate elements of the new style. These include complex love stories, paired characters such as lady and gallant or maid and sidekick, historically precise locations, varied versification, and special effects (McKendrick 134). His best-known dramatic texts are the tragedy *La destruición de Numancia*, which describes the futile resistance of that Iberian city to Roman colonizers, and the comic interlude *El retablo de las maravillas* (The Miracle Show), a satire of Spanish obsessions with honor, legitimacy, and "blood purity" that features village notables taken in by picaresque entertainers.

Although the interludes are available in English translation, and *Numancia* and *The Traffic of Algiers* were translated in 1870, Cervantes's other dramatic texts have never been translated. Yet they shed light both on the author's better known prose oeuvre and on crucial historical dynamics. With their own versions of irony, humor, and pathos, the plays offer another turn of the Cervantine kaleidoscope, demonstrating how whatever ideological forces shaped the author's corpus were necessarily altered by the constraints of genre, if not performance.

Given that these texts were not often performed, our sense of them does not depend as heavily on a performance history as is the case for the Shakespearean corpus, for example. Nonetheless, it is striking how closely Cervantes's prologue connects the material and performance history of Spanish drama with the texts produced by its playwrights. One example of this connection is the popularity of cross-dressing on the stage: although, unlike on the English stage, actresses were permitted, dramatists produced countless plays that required actresses to cross-dress, as such risqué plots were hugely popular with audiences. Thus Cervantes's *Bagnios of Algiers* includes a minor character, Ambrosio, whose main purpose seems to be the display of a famous actress, "Lady Catalina," in male attire.

Much of Cervantes's originality as a playwright lies in his Mediterranean subject matter. As his editors Florencio Sevilla Arroyo and Antonio Rey Hazas argue, Cervantes's plays on captivity "inaugurate a kind of theatrical mini-genre, the Barbary or Turkish captivity play, which he himself perfected and enriched" (Sevilla Arroyo and Rey Hazas 2:xi). This subgenre includes the early *Traffic of Algiers*, the two plays translated here, and *El gallardo español* (The Gallant Spaniard), also published in the 1615 volume. In this realm at least, Lope imitated Cervantes, with his 1599 play *Los cautivos de Argel* (The Captives of Algiers). Of the eight plays in the 1615 collection, we have chosen to translate two that offer very different Mediterranean locales and visions of captivity, *The Bagnios of Algiers* on North Africa and *The Great Sultana Doña Catalina de Oviedo* on the Ottoman court. Variously composed from direct experience and romance commonplaces, the two plays offer a window onto these fraught Mediterranean exchanges as imagined by Cervantes, himself a former captive. The frequent return to scenes of Algerian captivity and Ottoman pomp throughout Cervantes's oeuvre makes these plays essential documents for understanding both his historical context and his broader literary production.

Cervantes's Mediterranean

The Bagnios of Algiers and *The Great Sultana* enact the intense imaginative engagement of early modern Spain with the Muslim worlds of the Mediterranean. They also reflect Cervantes's first-hand experience of captivity in North Africa, which had a crucial impact on his writing. The religious and political rivalries on this "forgotten frontier," as Andrew Hess terms it (1978), serve as the backdrop to the complex set of relationships and identities explored in the texts.

The plays are set on the edge of two Mediterranean worlds that clashed repeatedly over the course of the sixteenth century, as a newly unified Spain rejected its Semitic heritage and faced the increasing threat of the Ottoman Empire and its North African protectorates. Yet the constant hostilities coexisted with regular contacts, commercial and otherwise. A steady stream of subjects crossed the line between these worlds, however unwillingly in some cases. Soldiers, merchants, exiles, captives, renegades—these often overlapping groups embody the complexity of the Mediterranean frontier. Identities and allegiances were frequently more complex than the rote recitation of historical facts might suggest. Cervantes's texts repeatedly underscore this complexity in the face of any ideological certainty, with unsettling effects.

The historical record indicates a recrudescence in relations between Spanish Christendom and the proximate world of Islam from the late fifteenth century, as Spain strained to consolidate as a "pure" Christian nation. The fall of Granada to the Catholic Monarchs in 1492 set the stage for an increasingly expansionist Spain in the years following, as the crusading fervor of campaigns on the peninsula was furthered on the coasts of the Maghreb. In the first decade of the sixteenth century, the Spanish conquered and looted a number of sites in North Africa—the Peñón de Vélez, Orán, Bougie, Tripoli—establishing isolated *presidios* (fortresses) that would become increasingly difficult to defend as the century wore on. Beyond immediate enrichment through conquest, the Spaniards sought to control the piracy based in the Barbary Coast. Repeated corsair attacks, such as the one depicted in *The Bagnios of Algiers*, devastated Spanish coastal settlements and took a tremendous toll in hostages.

These attacks were often enabled by Muslims who had been forced to leave Spain either during the war on Granada or during the subsequent suppression of Islamic belief. Though compelled to relocate to North Africa, these populations had a minute knowledge of their former homelands in southern Spain, as Cervantes's corsair Yzuf explains. Spanish speakers could often pass for Christians, which made them even more dangerous to unwitting ships or coastal towns. The situation was exacerbated over the course of Cervantes's lifetime, as many Moriscos (Muslims forced to convert to Christianity) and their descendants found refuge in North Africa. The years 1609–1614, the period of Cervantes's greatest productivity, saw the final expulsion of the Moriscos from Spain. This new wave of exiles, who had been Christians (however nominally in some cases) for multiple generations, also found its way to the Barbary Coast.

Beyond the Hispano-Muslim and Morisco exiles, many of the Barbary corsairs were of European origin, as renegades increasingly joined their ranks. Nor was piracy exclusively based in Algiers: the corsairs had their counterparts in Christian pirates and privateers, such as the Knights of Malta, who raided the Barbary Coast and beyond, looting and capturing hostages much as the Barbary corsairs did on European shores. On both sides of the Mediterranean, piracy furthered economic and geopolitical goals, serving as a "secondary form of war" between Christianity and Islam (Braudel 865). Yet in the early modern European literary imagination piracy was associated primarily with the North African corsair, a figure all the more troubling in that he was often a renegade.

The most famous and successful of the Barbary corsairs were the Barbarossa brothers, who in the first decades of the sixteenth century transformed Algiers into the strongest corsair base in the Mediterranean. Rallying his followers under the banner of Islam against the Spaniards, Arūj Barbarossa killed the ruler of Algiers and in 1516 proclaimed himself king of the city. He died fighting the Spaniards in 1518 and was promptly succeeded by his brother, Khair ad-Dīn, who cannily placed Algiers under the protection of the Ottoman Empire. Now nominally a protectorate, bolstered by Ottoman janissaries (elite infantry) and European renegades, Algiers became a powerful force in the western Mediterranean, launching bold attacks on Italian and Spanish coasts. Spanish control of North Africa became increasingly tenuous. In 1534, Barbarossa succeeded in capturing Tunis from the Spanish, although it was retaken a year later. In 1541, Emperor Charles V, king of Spain, assembled a massive fleet in order to attack Algiers, only to see it destroyed in a terrible storm—an episode that Cervantes possibly alludes to with the mirage of a fleet threatening the city in *Bagnios*. The balance of power thus shifted to favor the Ottomans and their client states, as conquest followed conquest: Tripoli was captured from the Knights of Malta in 1551, the island of Djerba in 1560, and the Venetian colony of Cyprus in 1570. The new Spanish ruler, Philip II, inherited from his father, Charles V, an increasingly complicated situation in the Mediterranean.

The Ottoman gains in the eastern Mediterranean and the growing power of Algiers in the west led to great anxiety in Europe. In response, Spain, Venice, and the Holy See formed an alliance against "the Turk" (the

Ottoman Empire), the Holy League. On October 7, 1571, under the command of Don Juan of Austria, illegitimate brother to Philip II, the great armada fought the Ottoman navy in the Gulf of Lepanto. On the galley *Marquesa* sailed the harquebusier Miguel de Cervantes, who acquitted himself with great courage despite being ill. The extraordinarily bloody battle ended in victory for the Holy League, albeit with heavy losses on both sides. Cervantes suffered severe wounds, leading to the loss of his left hand, whence his epithet, *el manco de Lepanto* (the one-handed man of Lepanto). He was extremely proud of his role in the battle and referred to it repeatedly in his writings. In the first part of *Don Quixote* (1605), the semiautobiographical character Ruy Pérez de Viedma, narrating his "Captive's Tale," describes his role in "that glorious battle . . . when Ottoman pride and arrogance were shattered" (Cervantes 2003, 337). The prologue to the second part of *Don Quixote* (1615) refers to Lepanto as "the greatest event seen in past or present times, or that future times can ever hope to see" (Cervantes 2003, 455).

▣ Captivity in Algiers ▣

Cervantes recovered from his wounds in Italy and served on a number of unsuccessful campaigns against the Ottomans. In 1575, he set sail for Spain, with letters of recommendation from Don Juan of Austria and the duke of Sessa to reward him for his heroic service at Lepanto. These would have ensured him a pension, had his voyage not come to a sorry end. Separated from its fellows by a storm, Cervantes's galley was attacked by Barbary corsairs off the Catalan coast. Along with the other survivors, including his brother Rodrigo, Cervantes was captured and taken to Algiers. There, the letters found on his person ensured that he would be treated with deference, as a *cautivo de rescate* (ransomable captive)—a valuable prize whose redemption could command a large sum. Given that Cervantes was in fact not a wealthy or well-connected man, his family could not come up with the enormous ransom of five hundred gold escudos demanded for his release.

Algiers in the 1570s was a tremendously cosmopolitan city, wealthy from privateering and the trade in captives, and thus much reviled in

Europe. Its reputation became somewhat of an overblown literary com-
monplace. The English travel writer Samuel Purchas colorfully described the city as "the Whirlepoole of these Seas, the Throne of Pyracie,
the Sinke of Trade and the Stinke of Slavery; the Cage of uncleane Birds
of Prey, the Habitation of Sea-Devils, the Receptacle of Renegadoes of
God, and Traytors to their Country" (*Hakluytus Posthumous or Purchas
His Pilgrimes*, 6:108f., qtd. in Chew 344). In his *Persiles*, Cervantes por-
trays false former captives who attract passersby with their sensational
account of the "glutton and devourer among all Mediterranean shores,
universal haven for corsairs, shelter and refuge for thieves" (Cervantes
1969, 344). Yet for early modern Spaniards captivity was not an exotic
possibility but a looming concern. As María Antonia Garcés notes,
"From the massive campaigns led by the ransomer monks to raise funds
for the rescue of captives, to the processions held when these ransomed
men and women returned home, to the chains and shackles hung in
churches and public buildings to signify liberation, the cruel reality of
captivity in Barbary was ever present for the Spaniards" (Garcés 172).

Unlike the false captives in his *Persiles*, Cervantes could draw on
his actual experience for a wealth of geographical and cultural details
on Algiers. His texts reflect the mix of subjects to be found in the city:
Muslims from throughout the Ottoman Empire, Moriscos from Spain,
Jews, Christians, and renegades of all stripes. When characters in Cervantes's Algiers refer to "Turks" and "Moors," these are not imprecise
catch-all terms for Muslims, as they often are in other European texts.
Instead, they generally reflect a precise understanding of the mix of peoples that populated Algiers in the later sixteenth century. Cervantes also
includes central historical figures in the city, many of whom he knew
first-hand, such as the powerful Ragusian renegade, Agi Morato (Hājjī
Murad, dates unknown) who served as an *alcaide* (governor) in Algiers
and conducted secret diplomatic missions for the Sultan in the 1570s;
Muley Maluco ('Abd al-Malik, 1541–1578), who ruled Fez and Morocco
from 1576 to 1578, and the renegade *beylerbey* (ruler) of Algiers himself,
Hazán Pasha (Hasan Pasha Veneziano, born 1545; ruled 1577–1581 and
1583–1585).

Cervantes spent his five years of captivity in the royal *bagnio*, or
prison, where the more valuable captives were kept. Less fortunate cap-

tives, who were not considered ransomable, belonged to the city and were forced to labor on public works or row in the galleys. In the royal bagnio, captives received better treatment, often through bribes, but they were not allowed to roam the city as were the city slaves. Priests were allowed to celebrate Mass for the captives, and on important holidays the services in the bagnio were open to all slaves, so long as they paid an entrance fee, as in the scene of Easter celebration depicted in *The Bagnios of Algiers*.

Despite his captors' threats, and conscious that he was being held for a ransom much higher than his family could possibly pay, Cervantes attempted escape on no fewer than four separate occasions. Surprisingly, although he did not manage to attain freedom, he was not punished for these attempts. Meanwhile, his family unsuccessfully tried to put together the ransoms for him and his brother through a series of loans. Rodrigo was ransomed first, in 1577, at his brother's urging. Miguel de Cervantes was finally freed in 1580 with help from the Trinitarians, one of the Spanish religious orders that ransomed captives in North Africa.

A View of "the Turk"

By contrast, Cervantes had no direct experience of Constantinople, where *The Great Sultana* is set, although the widespread European fascination with the Ottomans and their capital in the sixteenth century would have made familiar many of the stereotypes and commonplaces about "the Turk." In Spain, the most interesting text on the topic was the anonymous dialogue-cum-travel-narrative *El viaje de Turquía* (Travels to Turkey), probably composed around 1557, which used its sympathetic depictions of the Ottoman regime from the point of view of a captive to voice a humanist critique of Spanish venality and intolerance. The *Viaje*, which circulated in manuscript, reiterated many of the more common European perceptions of the Ottomans as they had appeared in multiple texts written by ambassadors, merchants, and other travelers to Constantinople. The harem, the janissaries, the sexual use of young boys, the justice system and its unusual punishments, all recur in depictions of the Ottomans in the period. More important, Cervantes's texts on the Ottomans—both the play included here and the novella "El amante liberal" (The Generous Lover)—share with the *Viaje* a distinctly humanist and cosmopolitan sensibility, in which the depiction of otherness obliquely reflects Spain's limitations.

Cervantes's plot of Sultan Amurates falling hopelessly for a Christian captive corresponds to Venetian ambassadors' account of Murad III (d. 1595) and his love for the Corfiote captive Safidje. Whereas *Bagnios*, a play set in North Africa and populated by Spanish captives and renegades, would hold an obvious appeal for his Spanish audience, Cervantes renders his Ottoman fantasy more proximate by making the irresistible captive a young Spanish girl, Catalina de Oviedo. Most striking in the play is the deflation of religious fervor: although the feisty Catalina is ready to become a martyr for her faith, there is no call for her to do so, as the Sultan is quite willing to tolerate her difference and respect her Christian belief. The Ottoman tolerance of religious minorities, even if they were carefully regulated and heavily taxed, would have seemed nothing short of miraculous to post-Reformation European audiences, more accustomed to the violent repression of confessional differences within Christianity as well as to a crusader rhetoric vis-à-vis Islam.

Forbidden Pleasures

The appeal of a play on the Ottomans, besides its vision of tolerance, lay primarily in its emphasis on "Oriental" sexual practices. Early modern European audiences were fascinated by Islamic polygyny and the imperial harem, by the eunuchs who served in the sultan's retinue, and especially by the Ottomans' love for boys. Historically, the captive women from the borders of the empire forced into the royal harem were valued prizes, symbols of Ottoman power, but in the European imagination they also signaled Ottoman excess. *The Great Sultana* puts the Sultan's many concubines on display, voyeuristically exposing that most secret and forbidden of spaces, the harem, and involving the audience in the ruler's choice of multiple sexual partners. It also suggests, in a somewhat farcical key, the considerable political power that the residents of the harem could exercise, and the emasculation of the Sultan through his erotic enthrallment.

Despite the strong disapproval of sodomy in Islamic law, amorous relations between mature men and subordinate boys were common in Ottoman aristocratic circles, as they were, to some extent, in absolutist European courts of the period (El-Rouayheb 3 and passim, Andrews and Kalpakli 17–18 and passim). While the young male beloved was the object of much passionate poetry in the Persian, Arabic, and Turkish traditions, it is by no means clear whether this idealizing rhetoric was connected with lust. Nonetheless, sodomy and pederasty became some of the most common stereotypes in the negative description of "Turks" or Moors by Europeans. Cervantes echoes these stereotypes in both plays with his frequent references to *garzones*—pageboys presumably available for sexual use by older men at court—and by suggesting that young male captives are at particular risk in both religious and sexual terms.

The plays also return repeatedly to the appeal of exogamous unions between those of different faiths. There is a particular frisson in the representation of Christian men in love with Moorish women, for although exogamous marriage was allowed for Muslim men so long as their wives were people of the book (Qur'an 5:5), it was forbidden for women (Qur'an 2:221). Although intermarriage was not unknown, a male captive's dalliance with his mistress, or even with a Muslim slave, could cost him his life. In his complex interweaving of romance plots, Cervantes exploits the transgressive appeal of such unions to the fullest.

▓ The Problem with Renegades ▓

The presence of religious minorities and interfaith unions did not mean that Algiers and Constantinople were neatly divided between captors and captives, Muslims and Christians. Part of what makes narratives of Mediterranean captivity so fascinating is the historical presence of renegades, who complicate any lines of allegiance or identity. *Topografia, e historia general de Argel*, a description of Algiers from the time of Cervantes, notes that more than half of its population were *turcos de profesión*, or professed Turks, as opposed to *turcos de nación*, or Turks by birth. The professed Turks, the *Topografía* explains, come from every corner of Europe and beyond, ranging from Muscovites to Albanians, from Scots to New World Indians (*Topografía*, 1:52, cited in Garcés 34–35). While literary accounts of renegades often emphasized their depravity and disregard for Christianity, the historical rationales for conversion to Islam were far more varied and complex. Many renegades were motivated by the greater social mobility, prosperity, and sophistication of North Africa or the Ottoman world when compared to a Europe that offered few possibilities for the dispossesed (Benassar and Benassar 419). A poor European sailor or apprentice could rise through the ranks much faster in these relatively meritocratic societies than he could at home, becoming a powerful janissary—a salaried member of the sultan's standing army—or a roving corsair captain. This was also the case for the boys forcibly conscripted through the *devshirmeh* (a system of human tribute to the Ottomans, primarily in the Balkans), converted to Islam, and trained for the janissary corps. Beyond their sheer numbers, the renegades also contributed important military and shipbuilding skills to the Ottomans. In *The Great Sultana*, the captive Madrigal taunts the Sultan with his vision of the ideal slaves: "My lord, would you rather this one were a smith, the other a shipbuilder, the third a gunpowder expert, or at least a master in artillery?" (Act I).

For both their actual contributions to Ottoman power and their perceived treachery to their faith, renegades were a source of great anxiety and profound fascination for early modern audiences. *The Bagnios of Algiers* presents two versions of the renegade—the traitor and the repentant martyr. Although the villainous Yzuf has clearly prospered as a corsair captain, the play condemns his betrayal of his native land, leaving aside any material rationale for his actions (or indeed, any sense of whether Yzuf chose his passage to North Africa or was forced there by Spanish exclusion). Meanwhile, the unfortunate Hazén, who apparently converted as a child, is desperate to return to Christianity and dies in the attempt. *The Great Sultana*, on the other hand, deflates the pathos and tension of the typical renegade plot, in that no one pressures the Spanish Christian Sultana to abandon her religion. The subplot of the captives Lamberto and Clara clearly shows the voluntary and interested embrace of Islam for political advancement, by characters safely located at a great remove from Spain.

Thus although both plays translated here are fundamentally concerned with captivity and the interactions between Christians and Muslims, their settings differ in important ways. While Cervantes had direct experience of Algiers, his notion of Constantinople was mediated by a highly conventional literature on "the Turk." Algiers represented for Spain a proximate threat, and was populated in part by voluntary and involuntary exiles from Spain, who complicated any notion of national belonging. While the depiction of Constantinople invoked the military threat of the Ottomans, its greater remove allowed for a more sustained exploration of tolerance as a considered imperial policy. Both plays feature a mix of historical specificity and literary license, with ideologically charged material—gender roles and exotic sexual practices, relations between the faiths, conversion to Christianity—clearly heightened.

⊕ The Plays ⊕

The two plays translated here were published in Cervantes's 1615 collection; they are generally assumed to have been written in the decade or so preceding publication. As Malveena McKendrick notes, both the 1601 reopening of the playhouses, which had closed to observe the death of Philip II, and the 1605 return of the Spanish court to Madrid after its sojourn in Valladolid would have led to an increased demand for plays (McKendrick 134), of which Cervantes unsuccessfully tried to take advantage. *The Bagnios of Algiers* reworks the themes of the earlier *Traffic of Algiers*, which Cervantes probably wrote in the early 1580s, shortly after his return from captivity. Its main plot, of a Spanish slave rescued by Zara, the beautiful and rich daughter of the renegade Agi Morato, forms the gist of the famous "Captive's Tale" in the first part of *Don Quixote*, in which she is called Zoraida. Both plays, as well as the Captive's story, draw heavily on Cervantes's own experience during captivity—he was

Hazán Pasha's captive during the period in which the story is set and thus knew Agi Morato as well as Zara/Zoraida.

Set almost entirely in Algiers, *The Bagnios of Algiers* features captors falling in love with their captives, and a lively cast of renegades. It opens with the renegade Hazén, who intends to return to Christianity and to Spain, collecting signatures from Christian captives who will vouch for his sincerity. Hazén's goodness and desire to reconvert to Christianity are contrasted to the perfidy of Yzuf, who leads a nocturnal attack on his native Spain. Captured in his raid are an old man and his two sons, Francisquito and Juanico; a ribald sexton, Tristán; and the beautiful Costanza, whose lover, Don Fernando, throws himself into the sea to follow her into captivity. The play also recounts the fantastic escape from Algiers to Spain of Zara, the rich daughter of Agi Morato—the plot that reappears in part 1 of *Don Quixote*.

The story of Zara and Lope the captive is both the most fanciful and the most historically specific in the play. Lope and his companions notice a pole dangling from a window over the bagnio. Attached to this marvelous pole are both money to buy the Spaniards' freedom and a letter from Zara, who informs Lope that she is Christian and wishes to escape with him to Spain. This munificent benefactor of romance is precisely identified as not only Agi Morato's daughter but also the intended of Muley Maluco (Abd-el Malik), who became the sultan of Morocco in 1576 and ruled until 1578.

Cervantes presents the life of the bagnio in great detail, including, on the one hand, the cruel punishments meted out to captives and, on the other, the surprising religious freedom they enjoyed, culminating in the representation of a *comedia* as part of Easter celebrations within the prison. *Bagnios* combines accurate descriptions of the conditions of captivity with flights of rhetorical fancy, to sometimes jarring effect. The text harnesses age-old romance motifs, often taken from the Byzantine novel, which embellish the workings of Mediterranean piracy and captivity: the travails of lovers separated by unforeseen circumstances, the erotic assault on a virtuous heroine by her captors, the unreliability and opacity of characters who exist between cultures and religions, and the marvelous escapes that ensure a protracted resolution.

The Bagnios of Algiers also presents an intriguing mix of Christian fervor and humanist skepticism. The sympathetic characters long for a return to liberty and Christianity, while the youngest captive, Francisquito, exultantly chooses martyrdom over conversion to Islam. He represents within the play the strongest version of Christian identity, and remains resistant to the lures of his master. Yet while his youth and vulnerability make him a highly sympathetic figure, his father's absolute willingness to see him martyred instead of converted introduces a jarring note. His brother Juanico's fate, meanwhile, is unclear—he simply disappears from the play after the end of Act II, but he does not escape to Spain with the other captives. Moreover, the character most closely connected to the Church in any formal sense, the sexton Tristán, is also the play's buffoon. He spends his time onstage torturing the Jews of Algiers, and forcing his victim to "ransom" from him everything from his Sabbath stew to his young child. While the Jews of the play are not particularly dignified or individualized—there is no Shylock here—Tristán's supposedly farcical infliction of the sufferings decried by Christian captives on his own scapegoat complicates any sense that the Christians are uniquely good or the Moors uniquely depraved. In fact, the Christians' appalling treatment of Jews makes the ordinariness of their existence in Algiers all the more striking. Moreover, Tristán's intimate familiarity with Jewish dietary law, which he exploits to blackmail the Jew, recalls how closely Spanish Jews and Christians had coexisted before the expulsion of the Jews from Spain in the name of religious purity in 1492.

The Moors are presented as cruel and unremittingly lustful: the captive boys become the object of their master's sodomical desire, while Costanza and Fernando are pursued by their respective master and mistress. Yet here too there are important exceptions: from the would-be counterrenegade Hazén, who is desperate to be back in Spain, to Zara, who is the daughter of a renegade and herself a secret Christian, things are not what they seem in the world of Algiers. The large number of characters whose religious allegiances are ambiguous suggests the impossibility of essentializing difference in a world full of renegades and counterrenegades. Even the most villainous of the Moors, Yzuf, complicates any simple view of the Mediterranean divide: he was born and raised in Spain, he tells us, and his violent attack on his former home is connected to his exile from it. And if, as the play insists, the captive boys and their father are related to Yzuf, then "Christian" piety and "Moorish" depravity exist within the same Morisco family (Irigoyen-García). Cervantes's stage direction *"Enter two or three young Moors, perhaps even taken from the street"* (Act II) suggests just how indistinguishable are the play's Moorish antagonists from its Christian, Spanish protagonists.

The Great Sultana, for its part, enacts an oxymoronic mixture of Turk and Christian in its very title—it is an Eastern tale with a Spanish Old Christian protagonist. The play tells the story of the young Spanish captive Catalina, who grows into a great beauty in the seraglio while hidden by a sympathetic renegade. Cervantes based the plot of *The Great Sultana* both on historical and on fictional sources. The former describe a Corfiote or Venetian Christian woman of whom Amurates III was enamored. Fictional sources with similar plotlines include the Byzantine novels of Achilles Tatius and Heliodorus, as well as stories by Italian authors such as Bandello and Cinthio (Cervantes 1998, 15: xiii). Since Cervantes himself never traveled to Turkey, he most likely relied on commonplaces about "the Turk," or perhaps a textual source such as *Viaje de Turquía*.

In *The Great Sultana*, Spanish identity is a constant theme. Catalina holds on to all the trappings of her Spanish self: her name, her dress, and, most important, her religion. The heroine's high Spanish virtues are matched in the low register by the wily *pícaro* (rogue) Madrigal, a Spanish captive who pokes fun at Muslims and Jews while trumpeting Spanish superiority. Despite his disdain for non-Christians, Madrigal tarries in Constantinople because of his own dalliance with a Moor, an unlawful adventure that almost gets him executed. Madrigal comes closest to an authorial figure in the play: he recounts Catalina's adventures in song to entertain the Sultan, and claims that on returning to Madrid he will become a playwright, the better to profit from his exotic experiences.

Sultan Amurates falls so completely in love with his Spanish captive that he decides to marry her, allowing her to remain a Christian and generally acceding to her requests. Under pressure from his advisers, who urge him to produce an heir as quickly as possible, he is forced to turn to others in his seraglio. Catalina triumphantly wins him back when she announces that she is already pregnant with his child—a future "Spanish Ottoman."

Meanwhile, a Hungarian captive, Lamberto, has cross-dressed to accompany his beloved Clara into the harem. Presented to the Sultan as a possible mother for his future heir, Lamberto reveals his true sex, to general horror. Yet he claims to have experienced a miracle, converting to Islam as a way to change his sex. Instead of punishing him, the Sultan rewards his blatantly opportunistic embrace of Islam with a military office. *The Great Sultana* thus resolves the contradictions of Mediterranean identity by, first, making hybridity a permanent condition in the next generation, and, second, underscoring the openness of the Ottoman Empire to those who would join it. The play has received considerable critical attention in the past decade, as scholars come to terms with its surprisingly benign version of Ottoman power. Although the Sultan seems to be completely emasculated by his love for Catalina, his canny appropriation of Spanish virtues and Hungarian manpower suggest an alternative model to Spanish imperial bravado.

The plots of both plays depend heavily on the erotic appeal of the other, nuancing complex questions of religious identity via the characters' often illicit attachments. Thus *The Great Sultana* features the striking exogamous union between the Sultan and Catalina but also, in a minor key, that between Madrigal and the anonymous Moor he desires. *The Bagnios of Algiers* anticipates the union of the captive Lope and his benefactor Zara—the Muslim daughter of a renegade, who herself wishes to become a Christian—while Muslim masters of both sexes lust after their Christian captives. When religion and eros conflict in exogamous unions, love qualifies conversion, just as conversion qualifies love.

Translations and Influence

Cervantes's vision of Algiers underlies many subsequent European representations of North African captivity, of renegades, and of the romantic fascination with religious others. As critics have noted, Cervantes was the first to bring the experience of captivity to Spanish theater, and his combination of historical specificity and romance fancy was quickly imitated. In England, *The Bagnios of Algiers* was appropriated and transformed in Philip Massinger's *The Renegado* (1623), and it clearly influenced other related plays, such as John Fletcher's *The Island Princess* (1621) and Thomas Heywood's *The Fair Maid of the West II* (1631). These texts trade in the recurring European fantasy of a Moorish woman's conversion to Christianity, sweetened by erotic attraction to the Christian protagonist. As we note above, this was a powerful literary diversion from the historical realities of captivity and the overwhelming frequency of conversion *to* Islam by Christian sailors, captives, and others.

The Bagnios is also an essential text to read in conjunction with the famous "Captive's Tale" in the first part of *Don Quixote*: it tells the same basic story but with important differences in its details, and with the addition of several interesting subplots among the renegades. While "The Captive's Tale" is the better known text, Cervantes offers in the play a number of alternative solutions, some of which are clearly determined by the dramatic genre. While there are, to the best of our knowledge, no explicit reworkings of *The Great Sultana*, its titillating vision of "the Turk" and his harem participates in the broader construction of an eroticized Orient in Cervantes's work and beyond.

▩ This Translation ▩

The basis for our translation is the most recent critical edition of the plays, coedited by Florencio Sevilla Arroyo and Antonio Rey Hazas, published in Alcalá in 1993 by Alianza and the Centro de Estudios Cervantinos. This solid edition corrects the errors in the original texts of the plays and provides variant readings from all the manuscripts as well as noting corrections by previous editors of the collection. The editors base their text on the original 1615 edition printed by the widow of Alonso Martín, who operated the latter's press after his death in 1614, five contemporary copies of which were consulted in the Spanish National Library in Madrid; the editors also employed a facsimile edition made in 1984 by the Spanish Royal Academy. Because we are dealing with a regularized and critically edited text, we have not faced significant problems of variant readings. We have signaled the occasional emendation to the text in our footnotes.

Since our intention is to provide a text for study rather than for performance, we have opted for a prose translation of the plays, which has allowed us to remain as close as possible to Cervantes's language. That said, every effort has been made to keep the translations and stage directions faithful to contemporary performance. Our annotation directs the reader to pertinent studies or historical information necessary for a better understanding of the plays.

▣ A Note on Coins ▣

Characters in Cervantes's plays mention a variety of coins. Though mainly Spanish, there is also mention of the *áspero*, a coin of lesser value that circulated under Ottoman rule throughout the Levant. As Spanish coinage under the Habsburgs was a somewhat complicated system not based on simple equivalency, we provide a list of coins below. Coin values changed markedly over time, so our list is relative. Denominations are listed in descending order of value. For reference, according to a contemporary reformist writer, a poor man in 1620 would spend 30 maravedís daily (Elliott 2002, 286), or 30 escudos in a year. Cervantes's ransom was an exorbitant 500 escudos (Garcés 28).

$$
\begin{aligned}
1 \text{ gold escudo} &= 350\text{–}400 \text{ maravedís} \\
1 \text{ silver escudo} &= 12 \text{ reales, } 100 \text{ ásperos} \\
1 \text{ ducado (ducat)} &= 11 \text{ reales, } 375\text{–}429 \text{ maravedís} \\
1 \text{ dobla} &= 6 \text{ reales, } 50 \text{ ásperos} \\
1 \text{ real} &= 34\text{–}50 \text{ maravedís, } 10\text{–}12 \text{ ásperos}
\end{aligned}
$$

The Bagnios of Algiers

DRAMATIS PERSONAE[1]

CAURALÍ, *Captain of Algiers*

YZUF, *a renegade*

FIRST MOOR

SECOND MOOR

THIRD MOOR

FOURTH MOOR

An OLD MAN

JUANICO, *his son*

FRANCISQUITO, *his son*

TRISTÁN, *a* SEXTON

COSTANZA, *a Christian woman*

A CHRISTIAN CAPTAIN

TWO CHRISTIAN HARQUEBUSIERS

DON FERNANDO

WARDEN PASHA

DON LOPE, *a captive*

VIVANCO, *a captive*

JULIO, *a captive*

HAZÉN, *a renegade*

CARAHOJA, *a Moor*

HAZÁN PASHA, *king of Algiers*

CADÍ

ALIMA, *a Moor*

ZARA, *a Moor*

THREE YOUNG MOORS

AMBROSIO, *who is played by* LADY CATALINA[2]

A JEW

OSORIO

GUILLERMO, *a shepherd*

BOAT CAPTAIN

---

1. Our list of the dramatis personae comes from the first printed edition, dated 1615, with some editorial modifications. We have regularized Zara's name, included the Sexton's name, and inserted the two characters not found in the original list that appears in the play: Julio and the Boat Captain.

2. This "Lady Catalina" is usually identified as Catalina Hernández Verdeseca, a famous contemporary actress, who was the wife of the theater manager and actor Gaspar de Porres.

Act I

[*Enter* CAURALÍ, *Captain of Algiers;* YZUF, *renegade; and four other* MOORS, *named* FIRST, SECOND, THIRD, *and* FOURTH MOORS.]

YZUF.

Come quietly one by one, for this is the path and this is the village. Keep to the woods.

CAURALÍ.

Make no mistake, Yzuf, for an error may cost you your life.

YZUF.

Don't worry; have the people get their swords and torches ready.

CAURALÍ.

Have you decided from where we should attack, Yzuf?

YZUF.

From the mountains, a place so impassable it is unguarded. As I said, I was born and raised in this land, and I know well its ins and outs and the best places to make war on it.

CAURALÍ.

The ladders are ready now, and so far the sentries are distracted with drink or sleep.

YZUF.

Dawn's eyes must not find us here.

CAURALÍ.

You are our all: lead us, attack, and triumph!

YZUF.

May it be so. Don't stray in the least from the orders I've given, for that way I shall give you victory before any assistance arrives.

[*Exeunt. Shouts of* MOORS *are heard within; torches are lit, the village is set afire, and an* OLD MAN *comes to the wall half naked and says.*]

OLD MAN.

God save me! What is this? Moors on land? We are lost! Friends, you're being destroyed! To arms, to arms! This time the coast guard's diligence has been foiled; the sentries sleep, all is slumber. O, if only I

could carry my dear sons, like a Christian Aeneas, away from this con-
flagration to a safe light! Is there no one to sound the alarm? No one to
ring those silent bells to pieces? I'm coming to help you, beloved sons!

[*Exit. The* SEXTON *comes to the wall, wearing an old soutane
and a head wrap.*]

SEXTON.

It's the Turks,[1] after all. O tower, my defense! You trump the sacristy
on this occasion. I must ring the bells and quickly sound the alarm
[*he rings the bell*]; my heart is losing its courage and I'm dying of fear.
No guard on the shore has lit any beacon—a sure sign of our ruin.
As a man of the cloth, and no workman, I can ring a clapper better
than I can unsheathe a sword.

[*He rings again and exits.* CAURALÍ *and* YZUF *enter
with two other* MOORS.]

YZUF.

Those who attempt to take refuge in the mountains will come this
way, no doubt; wait, and you'll see fearful and silent people coming to save themselves. Before any help arrives, we would do well to
withdraw.

CAURALÍ.

Are the vessels close by on the shore?

YZUF.

Loaded for our pleasure and our shame.

[*Exeunt. The* OLD MAN *enters carrying a half-naked small child
and leading another by the hand.*]

OLD MAN.

Where shall I take you, living tokens of my dead heart? I would
rather see you in narrow graves than have you captured.

CAURALÍ.

My sword will relieve you of your pensive speeches, giving you life
for my greater fortune, rather than seeking the pleasure of your
death.

---

1. In the confusion of the raid, the distinction between "Moors" and "Turks" disappears.
There were close connections between the Barbary States and the Ottomans in Cervantes's
time, as Algiers was an Ottoman regency. Other North African regions such as Tunis and
Tripoli were subordinate to the Algerian pasha, or regent (Friedman 9).

FRANCISQUITO.

Father, why did you take me from bed? I'm freezing to death! Where
are we going? Pick me up, like my brother. Why are we up so early?

OLD MAN.

O branches of this useless and ruined trunk, so tender, loving, and
fine! I know not where I'm going; though it is clear the end of this
road will be my death.

CAURALÍ.

Bairán,[2] take them to the shore, and make sure the fleet is ready, for,
as the Horn[3] tells you, Tithonus's wife draws near.[4]

[*The* OLD MAN *exits, the* SEXTON *enters.*][5]

OLD MAN.

It's useless to flee from the woe that heaven decrees.

SEXTON.

I suspect—if heaven does not help my wits—that I was safer in my
tower. Who tricked me? And worse still if I should miss the road or
shortcut to the mountain.

CAURALÍ.

Walk to the shore, you dog!

SEXTON.

Dog? Now I know my mother was a bitch.

CAURALÍ.

Hurry along with him, and have the flagship set sail and follow the
coast to the cove where we anchored.

[*Exeunt the* FIRST MOOR *and* SEXTON.]

YZUF.

What did you say, Cauralí?

---

2. Bairán, a renegade, figures in the dramatis personae of *El gallardo español* (The Gallant Spaniard), another captivity play by Cervantes with themes similar to the ones in this
volume.

3. The Horn in this passage (in Spanish, *la bocina*) refers to the constellation Ursa Minor
(the Little Dipper), not an actual horn.

4. The reference here is to Aurora, the dawn, wife of Tithonus in Greek mythology.

5. Here, as at several points throughout the plays, characters exit while uttering a few ad-
ditional lines (perhaps on their way offstage). We have maintained the placement of the stage
directions of the Spanish original.

SECOND MOOR.

I can't say.

YZUF.

Listen, Cauralí, I think I heard a trumpet sound.

CAURALÍ.

Your fear, no doubt, makes the sound that throws your courage into turmoil.

YZUF.

Sound the retreat, for dawn is here, your fleet is full of booty, and I think reinforcements are approaching. To the shore!

CAURALÍ.

Everyone to the shore!

[*Exeunt. A trumpet sounds; four* MOORS *enter, one after another, laden with booty.*]

FIRST MOOR.

Although the booty is scant, it's valuable.

SECOND MOOR.

I don't know what I'm carrying, but oh well.

THIRD MOOR.

What we've done so far has been well done.

FOURTH MOOR.

May Allah grant us an empty beach!

[*A* MOOR *enters with a damsel named* COSTANZA, *who is half naked.*]

COSTANZA.

My heart is pounding in my breast, I'm out of breath and faint of heart. Lead me more slowly.

MOOR.

Hurry, bitch, for the sea awaits you!

COSTANZA.

Farewell, my heaven and earth!

[COSTANZA *exits; a* CHRISTIAN *comes to the wall.*]

CHRISTIAN.

To the shore, to the shore, friends, for the Turks hasten to embark! If you hurry, our enemies will abandon their booty, sadly lost and unfairly won.

[*A* CHRISTIAN HARQUEBUSIER *enters.*]

FIRST HARQUEBUSIER.

We can only bear witness that here was Troy.[6]

SECOND HARQUEBUSIER.

O perverse Fortune, give wings to my feet, fire to my hands!

FIRST HARQUEBUSIER.

Our efforts are in vain, for the Turks have already embarked and coast along near the shore.

[*The* CHRISTIAN CAPTAIN *enters.*]

CAPTAIN.

Oh! Curse my feet, more used to rocky cliffs than to the sand! What happened to the horse guard?[7]

FIRST HARQUEBUSIER.

The horsemen arrived on the beach exhausted just as the galleys set sail, and after them came three companies. I found the two sentries dead, from gunshot wounds, I think. The darkness absolves the sentries of the miserable scene I behold.

SECOND HARQUEBUSIER.

What should we do?

CAPTAIN.

Take a detour through the woods, and hide in the neighboring cove, to see what the corsair intends.

FIRST HARQUEBUSIER.

What can he intend but to return to Algiers, given that he's got what he came for?

CAPTAIN.

Who would dare attempt such a great feat?

SECOND HARQUEBUSIER.

If it's Morato Arráez,[8] he's truly daring; all the more so as he was probably brought here by some renegade familiar with this land.

---

6. The Spanish expression *aquí fue Troya* was frequently used in the period to denote ruinous defeat, failure, or lost grandeur (Covarrubias 979, s.v. *Troia*).

7. The horse guard mentioned here was charged with protecting Spanish coasts from pirate attacks and sounding an early alarm.

8. Morato Arráez was a famed renegade corsair originally from Albania and a common reference in the period. He also figures in Act I of *The Great Sultana* as the Sultana's original captor.

CAPTAIN.

There's one from here who's unmatched as a traitor. Where's my brother?

FIRST HARQUEBUSIER.

He had no sooner arrived than, terrified and breathless, he dashed to the village.

CAPTAIN.

He'll find a sad start to the wedding he longed for.

[DON FERNANDO *appears on the wall.*]

FERNANDO.

Towers of clear crystal, instead of battlements, walls of rich and burnished silver that once sheltered my hope, tell me: where, oh where, might I find my Costanza? Roofs that vomit torchlike flames, streets flowing with blood and tears, where is the cause of my now uncertain glory and of my certain grief? Reveal, o sun, your shining tresses; open, Aurora, your rosy portals; let me glimpse the sea, on which sails the good that heaven denies me for my sins.

CAPTAIN.

Let's go help him, lest he take his own life;[9] for his words suggest he's gone mad.

FIRST HARQUEBUSIER.

You're right; let's go, for his malady requires a strong and swift charm.

[*Exeunt.*]

FERNANDO.

Yet what am I saying, o wretch! I can see clearly from the traces of this evildoing that my dearly beloved has been taken captive, and I must try to free her.

[DON FERNANDO *exits; the* CAPTAIN *appears on the wall with another soldier.*]

I will signal from that high cliff; perhaps the vile Moor will want to exchange money for the beauty no treasure could buy.

---

9. The Spanish verb *desesperar* had connotations of both "losing hope" and "commiting suicide" in Cervantes's time, both in Spanish and in English. Cf. Shakespeare's *Hamlet*: "The very place puts toys of desperation, / Without more motive, into every brain / That looks so many fathoms to the sea / And hears it roar beneath" (I.iv.75–79).

CAPTAIN.

My brother is no longer here; I fear his fierce sorrow may destroy the
dignity befitting who he is. What an extraordinary affair!

FIRST HARQUEBUSIER.

Sir, he's over there, if I'm not mistaken.

[*Exit the* CAPTAIN; *enter* DON FERNANDO, *climbing up a crag.*]

FERNANDO.

Climb, o tired feet! Reach the peak of this rocky rugged land, if the
immense weight of my cares does not hold you in this thicket. Now I
glimpse that frightful contraption, swiftly making off with my heavenly cargo in its awful devouring bowels; now it spreads its wings, now
its limbs assist it, now it sets its course. This signal I send—of ransom,
peace, and alliance—is useless, nor will my voice, though I shout,
reach as far as my desire. Ah, my beloved Costanza! Ah, sweet, honored wife! Do not listen to the pleas of unbelievers or give in to powerful Hagarene[10] force, for I still have life for the journey! Come back,
come back, tyrants! I offer to sate your greedy hearts with pleasure
and glory, and my hands, strangers to avarice, will doubtless augment
your victory. Come back, for all your plunder is vile dross compared
to the rich gifts I bestow in exchange for my sun, eclipsed among
the dark clouds that you, gentle north wind, raise from the sea. All
the gold of Arabia, all the pearls of the South, and the most precious
Tyrean purple I generously grant you, although they might be cum-
bersome to own. If you return my wife, I offer you a new world, with
all that heaven and earth contain. I'm out of my mind—but since I am
not worthy of this glory, take my body, for you take my soul.

[*He hurls himself from the cliff.*]

[*Enter* WARDEN PASHA[11] *and a* CAPTIVE *with ink and paper.*]

WARDEN.

Hey! Get to work, Christians! Nobody stay inside; ill or hale, don't

10. Hagarene (*agarena* in the original) literally means a descendant of the biblical Hagar,
Abraham's other wife and mother of Ishmael; by extension, an Arab or Muslim.

11. The principal warden of the bagnio was known as the *guardián bají* (warden pasha), with
several assistants under him, usually janissaries (Friedman 61). The title "Pasha" was the highest honorific in the Ottoman Empire (*OED*).

delay, for if I go in there, these hands will get you on your feet. I want everyone, priest or nobleman, to work. Hey, dirty swine! Must I call you again?

[*A* CAPTIVE *enters, and those that are able come out one by one.*]

CAPTIVE.

I want to be the first.

WARDEN.

This one to the woodpile, this one to the docks; keep good track of everything; send thirty to that *burche*[12] and sixty to the wall; twenty to the brick kiln and ten to Caralí's house. And hurry, the day flies by!

SLAVE.

The Cadí[13] sent for forty; courtesy demands we give them to him.

WARDEN.

Necessity, too. Don't worry about that; send two more like them to the bricks, as you did yesterday.

SLAVE.

There would be something for everyone to do, even if there were two thousand of them. Where should the gentlemen go?

WARDEN.

Leave them for tomorrow, for they'll be the first.

SLAVE.

And if they pay?

WARDEN.

It's obvious that where there's money there's rest.

SLAVE.

I'll befriend them so that you can get your way and a goodly sum.

WARDEN.

Send out the skilled workers.

SLAVE.

I shall. God be with you.

[*Exeunt. Enter* DON LOPE *and* VIVANCO, *captives, their feet in chains.*]

---

12. In one of many touches of local color, Cervantes uses the word *burche*, from the Arabic *borch*, for a tower or castle.

13. The Cadí served as both bishop and judge in Muslim polities.

LOPE.

It was no small blessing to escape from the work in store for us today.

VIVANCO.

When I don't work, I'm even more tired and fatigued. For me this close confinement is an awful torture, and seeing the fields or the sea relieves me.

LOPE.

For me the sight of them is torture, for the melancholy in my soul from my lack of liberty prefers unhappy solitude to joyful company. It's plain to see that working and not eating are the first steps toward death.

[*Enter a Christian* CAPTIVE, *fleeing from the* WARDEN, *who follows behind and beats him.*]

WARDEN.

O *chufetre!*[14] Must you always hide like this? You must have been spoiled as a child, useless dog.

CAPTIVE.

For God's sake, Effendi,[15] I'm sick!

WARDEN.

Well, I'll cure you straightaway by sweating you with this stick.

CAPTIVE.

For more than two days I've been running a fever that confuses and bewilders me.

WARDEN.

And that's why you were hiding?

CAPTIVE.

Yes, Effendi.

WARDEN.

Get going, dog!

[*As they exit, the guard continues to beat the captive.*]

LOPE.

By God, the wretch he's beating is a good soldier—he's not dissembling!

14. *Chufetre*, from the Turkish *chefet*, was an insult equivalent to "infidel" or "dog."
15. Turkish, "Master."

VIVANCO.

Well, look at what remedy he's found in his illness. Isn't it absurd
that even when a captive's close to death they won't believe him?
And when they see him dead they say: "G'Allah,[16] the wretch must
have been sick!" O false swine, wholly bereft of mercy! Who resorts
to lies when he's losing his life? Death is the best witness of how we
suffer for your incredulity; you believe a dead man over the most
truthful one alive.

LOPE.

Raise your eyes and look over there, Vivanco, and see if you spot a
white handkerchief that hangs from a long pole.

[*A pole appears, with a bulging white handkerchief tied to it.*]

VIVANCO.

You're right, and it's knotted up. I want to go over there to see this
feat. By God, the pole rises!

LOPE.

Go to it, perhaps it will drop.

VIVANCO.

This adventure isn't for me, Don Lope; you come try it, for something
tells me your fortune will reach for it.

LOPE.

Some lad must have set bait or traps there to hunt swifts.

VIVANCO.

It's not deep or far; come, and we'll soon see. Don't you see how the
pole leans toward you? My God, this is a marvel!

LOPE.

There is a prize inside the cloth.

VIVANCO.

If it's a prize, untie it straight away.

LOPE.

It's eleven gold escudos; among them a doubloon that's like the Our
Father to this rosary.[17]

---

16. G'Allah: from the Spanish *gualá*, from the Arabic *wallá[h]*, "by God."

17. Rosaries are often organized into "decades" of ten beads representing Hail Marys and a
larger bead for the Our Father.

VIVANCO.

An excellent analogy!

LOPE.

The pole has lifted again. What manna from heaven is this? What Habbakuk has come to our prison to give us this basket filled with something better than food?[18]

VIVANCO.

Don Lope, why don't you go and greet and thank the author of this deed? O pole, from now on no longer pole but staff of virtues!

LOPE.

Whom do you want me to thank, if I can't see anyone through that lattice?

VIVANCO.

Well, someone must have sent this.

LOPE.

Of course, but I don't know who. Perhaps a renegade Christian woman who likes to show compassion, or a captive Christian locked in that house. Yet whoever she is, she should see us looking thankful: bow to her two thousand times so that she believes our intent; I'll bow in the Moorish fashion in case it was a Moorish woman who favored us.[19]

[*Enter the renegade* HAZÉN.]

LOPE.

Quiet—Hazén is coming.

VIVANCO.

Cursed be the hour that brings that d—! I swallow the *o* and the *g* against my will.

LOPE.

God! I think he heard you.

18. Habbakuk brought bread to Daniel in the lion's den, according to Daniel 14:33 in the Latin Vulgate Bible. The story comes from the story of Bel and the Dragon, a chapter of Daniel not included in all Christian versions of the book.

19. The "Moorish ceremonies" referred to here allude to *zalemas*, which were ritual bows by an inferior to a superior person (Covarrubias 391, s.v. *çalema*).

VIVANCO.

If he did hear me, by God, it was good that I didn't finish his name.

HAZÉN.

With just your two signatures I'll happily set foot on Spanish shores;
I'll have a favorable wind, a calm sea with smooth waves. I want to
return to Spain, and to one to whom I must confess my childish and
ancient error, not like Yzuf, that dog who went back to sell out his
village.

[*He gives them a handwritten note.*]

It states here that it is true that I have treated Christians very affably,
without Turkish cruelty in word or deed; that I have aided many; that,
as a child, I was compelled to turn Turk; that, though I go roving,[20]
I am a good Christian underneath.[21] Perhaps I'll have a chance to
remain in what for me is the Promised Land.

LOPE.

When the sinner mends his ways, he pays an advance on his own salvation. We'll happily provide the signatures you ask of us, for we have
witnessed that all you say is true, Hazén, and that you are honest.

May heaven grant that your course be as smooth as you desire.

VIVANCO.

You're determined to do great things.

HAZÉN.

I'm determined to do even more, for I will try to raise a mutiny on
my galliot.

LOPE.

How do you plan to do it?

HAZÉN.

I've already arranged it with four others.

---

20. The Spanish phrase *ir en corso* is equivalent to early modern English "to rove," meaning
to practice piracy. The first appearance of the verb "to rove" is in 1548, according to the *OED*.

21. Renegades wishing to return to Christianity and to Spain were required to prove their
religious conviction to the Inquisition and to undergo a formal investigation before being "rec-
onciled" with the church. The signatures that Hazén is collecting would serve as evidence for
making his case. We have translated the original *oprimido a ser turco* with the idiomatic expression "to turn Turk" because of its frequent use in early modern English plays, many of which
are similarly preoccupied with religious renegades.

VIVANCO.

I fear treachery[22] if many know about this, for in Algiers nothing is ever achieved without struggle when many are told.

HAZÉN.

Those I speak of can be trusted with this and more.

LOPE.

Could you tell us, Hazén, who lives in that house over there?

HAZÉN.

That one?

VIVANCO.

Yes.

HAZÉN.

Certainly. A Moor of fine disposition, a good and notable man, and extremely rich. Beyond all else, Heaven has given him such a daughter that all the wealth of beauty is numbered in her.[23] Muley Maluco[24] longs to marry her.

LOPE.

And the Moor, what does he say?

HAZÉN.

That he deserves her, not for being a king, but for the gold that he offers as dowry: for in this strange nation, it's customary for the husband to pay the dowry, not the wife.[25]

---

22. We have translated *azar* as "treachery" here, for though the word could also be translated as "bad luck" or "mischance," in this situation it clearly has the connotation that someone will betray Hazén and thus ruin his plan, as Arroyo and Hazas note in their edition (Cervantes 1998, 14:40).

23. Agi Morato (Hājjiī Murad) was a renegade and emissary of the Sultan, called Hajji for having completed the pilgrimage to Mecca, the hajj. He was from Ragusa (Dubrovnik) in modern-day Croatia (Garcés 51). Morato was instrumental in beginning what would become the truce negotiations between Spain and the Ottoman Empire from 1579 to 1581. He is mentioned in *Don Quixote* part 1, chapter 40, as "a very prominent and wealthy Moor...who had been the governor of La Pata, which is a very distinguished position among those people" (Cervantes 2005, 345-46). His daughter, Zara, marries Don Lope and escapes to Spain with him; this escape is recounted in great detail in *Don Quixote*, part 1, chapters 40 and 41, where Morato himself makes a dramatic appearance that is totally absent from the *Bagnios*. His house was "one of the most luxurious of the city" (Garcés 208).

24. Muley Maluco ('Abd al-Malik), to whom the real-life Zara was engaged, became the sultan of Morocco in 1576 and ruled until 1578.

25. This dowry, or *mahr*, is paid in cash or property to the wife or her family and must be present in order for the marriage to be valid, according to classical Islamic jurisprudence.

VIVANCO.

And does she share her father's opinion?

HAZÉN.

She does not refuse him.

LOPE.

Is there perhaps a slave woman, renegade or Christian, in this house?

HAZÉN.

There was one years ago named Juana. Yes, yes—Juana was her name, and her last name, I think, was Rentería.

LOPE.

What became of her?

HAZÉN.

She's dead now, but she raised that Moorish woman of whom I told you earlier. She was a great matron, a paragon of Christianity, queen of the captives; there's no one as good in this city now. We renegades lament her absence, for we are blind without her light and counsel. In taking her back, heaven caused her masters a great loss.

LOPE.

Go in peace, and come for your signatures this afternoon, Hazén.

[HAZÉN exits.]

HAZÉN.

May the whole Trinity keep you.

VIVANCO [*looking at money*].

We could recount our good fortune. How many were there?

LOPE.

Didn't I say eleven? But what pains me is not to see who gave them.

VIVANCO.

Who? I think it was He who rules heaven, who in unforeseen ways reaches His generous hand out to miserable wretches and so helps us, although we're unworthy of such grace.

[*The pole appears again, with a larger handkerchief.*]

Look, the pole comes out once more.

LOPE.

Trouble yourself to go and see if it leans your way.

VIVANCO.

This is divine fishing, even if it's Mohammedan. Yet I scarcely move my foot and they raise the pole. I don't know why; if they're scared of me, let them say it and I'll turn back. For you, friend, this fine fortune lies waiting. Come, let's see what it is, and don't drag your feet, for when fortune comes, it doesn't tarry.

[*The pole bends toward* DON LOPE, *and he unties the handkerchief.*]

LOPE.

I think this one weighs more than the last.

VIVANCO.

It must have more money.

LOPE.

No, no—this is a note!

VIVANCO.

You want to read it now? See if it has any gold or silver first, for I'm about to burst with joy. Don't you want to look?

[DON LOPE *begins to read the note, and before finishing it, says:*]

LOPE.

By God, there's more than a hundred, and most are doubloons![26]

VIVANCO.

Why do you stop to read? Hurry up and count them.

LOPE.

Truly, this is the rarest of rare adventures.

VIVANCO.

What does the note say?

LOPE.

In what little I've read, I've seen miracles.

VIVANCO.

Listen, I hear something.

LOPE.

People are rushing in—let's get into the mess, where we can see what the letter says undisturbed.

---

26. See the Introduction for an explanation of coins.

VIVANCO.

Did you say goodbye?

LOPE.

I did.

VIVANCO.

Someone's ears have been cut off.[27]

[*Enter the* WARDEN *and a Moor named* CARAHOJA *and a* CHRISTIAN
whose ears are tied with bloody rags, as though they've been cut off.]

CARAHOJA.

Didn't I tell you, stupid dog, that I would do this to you if you fled by
land?

CHRISTIAN.

Liberty is enticing.

CARAHOJA.

You ingrate! I told you to escape by sea; but you, scoundrel, don't
care about the obstacles and always try to escape by land.

CHRISTIAN.

Until I'm dead and buried.

CARAHOJA.

This dog has fled thrice by land, and I gave thirty doubloons to those
who brought him back.

CHRISTIAN.

If you don't double[28] my chains, you should just pretend you've lost
me. for even if you lop me off all around and leave me worse off than
I already am, I so want to be free that I'll flee by land, air, water, and
fire. On the lookout for liberty, I will try anything that promises this
pleasure. And though it may enrage you all the more, I'll answer
your claim that you cut short my escape: it makes no difference
when you cut the branch if you do not tear out the roots. If you don't
cut off my feet, nothing can stand in the way of my escape.

WARDEN.

Carahoja, isn't this one a Spaniard?

---

27. Friedman notes that this was a common punishment for galley slaves under both Ottoman and European rule (73–74).

28. The captive puns on the senses of *doblas* as "double" and "doubloon."

CARAHOJA.

Isn't it obvious? Can't you tell from his courage?

WARDEN.

By Allah, even if he were dead you couldn't be sure of keeping him. Dog, get to the infirmary! You'll have to set this one to begging.

CARAHOJA.

It's true.

[*The* CHRISTIAN *exits.*]

WARDEN.

Listen—they've fired a shot at sea.

CARAHOJA.

I didn't hear it.

[*A* CAPTIVE *enters.*]

CAPTIVE.

Effendi, Cauralí has arrived, and he comes, as I've heard, rich, prosperous, and honored; the king is going to the shore to examine the captives and booty.

WARDEN.

Do you want to come?

CARAHOJA.

I'm limping.

WARDEN.

So walk slowly.

[*Exeunt.* DON LOPE *and* VIVANCO *reenter.*]

VIVANCO.

Read it again, for its simplicity and daring astound me.

LOPE.

See if anyone is coming, and move back to this side. This is what the letter says—I haven't seen such plain reasoning in my life. These are your wonders, o Lord!

VIVANCO.

Hurry up and tell me.

LOPE [*reading the letter*].

"My father, who is very rich, had a Christian woman captive, who nursed me and taught me everything Christian. I know the four prayers,[29] and can read and write—this is my handwriting. The Christian woman told me that Lela Marién, whom you call Saint Mary, loved me dearly, and that a Christian would take me to his land. I've seen many in this bagnio through the holes of this lattice, and none has seemed right except for you. I am beautiful, and have much of my father's money in my power. If you agree, I'll give you enough to ransom yourself, and you find a way to take me to your country, where you shall marry me; and if you don't want to, I won't really care, for Lela Marién will provide a husband for me. You may answer with the pole when the bagnio is empty. Send word of your name, where you are from, and whether you're married, and don't trust any Moor or renegade. My name is Zara, and may Allah keep you." [To VIVANCO] What do you think?

VIVANCO.

That heaven shows itself on earth in this most holy fervor.

LOPE.

Without a doubt, Zara holds all that is good in the world.

VIVANCO.

Perhaps she's watching us. Go back and give signs of gratitude from time to time. What is holding you back?

LOPE.

I'm thinking of a response.

VIVANCO.

What shall you respond but that you'll do everything necessary?

[HAZÉN enters.]

LOPE.

Hazén is coming back.

HAZÉN.

I so value the favor you will do for me that I cannot rest until I have it in my possession. [LOPE returns the note to him with the signatures.]

LOPE.

Friend Hazén, it's all done; may it serve you as much as it pleases me to do it.

---

29. These four prayers—cornerstones of Catholic orthodoxy after the Council of Trent—were the Hail Mary, the Our Father, the *Salve Regina* (Hail Holy Queen), and the Credo.

VIVANCO.

Is it true that Caralí is here?

HAZÉN.

He's already been seen from the Cape of Metafús.

LOPE.

What are you thinking about?

HAZÉN.

Now, to it! I'll find the renegade and tell him to his face what he is.

VIVANCO.

Do you mean Yzuf?

HAZÉN.

Yes, that ruthless dog.

LOPE.

A quarrel with him will do you no good.

VIVANCO.

Leave him alone; may God curse him!

HAZÉN.

My soul winces at seeing that infamous dog sell out and spill his own blood as though it were his foe's. May God help me, and be with you as well, for you'll never see me again. May God grant you freedom.

VIVANCO.

Be careful what you do, Hazén!

[*Exit* HAZÉN.]

HAZÉN.

God moves my will!

VIVANCO.

Do you wager his fury will make him quarrel with Yzuf?

LOPE.

I wish he would finish him off, to strike that lightning bolt of Mohammed from the earth. But shouldn't we write, in case this star we watch appears again?

VIVANCO.

I think so too—right away.

LOPE.

Let's go.

VIVANCO.

Let's.

[*Exeunt. Enter* HAZÁN PASHA,[30] *King of Algiers, the* CADÍ, *and* CARAHOJA, HAZÉN, *the* WARDEN, *and other* MOORS *in their retinue; shawms*[31] *and cries sound at their arrival.*]

PASHA.

Cauralí comes in high spirits! What do you think, Warden?

WARDEN.

His cleverness and strength always lead to this; he's bold, and he had a brave renegade to guide him.

PASHA.

Wasn't it Yzuf?

WARDEN.

Yes, it was Yzuf, whom fame proclaims a good Moor and good soldier.

[*Enter* CAURALÍ *and* YZUF.]

CAURALÍ.

Let me kiss your feet, brave Hazán, as my king and my lord.

PASHA.

My feet are not for such brave lips or for such a bold captain. Get up.

YZUF.

You'll give me what you so rightly deny Cauralí.

PASHA.

My arms are open for both of you.

CADÍ.

And the Cadí's as well. Welcome.

CAURALÍ.

I wish you the same.

---

30. Hasan Pasha, or Hasan Veneziano, was a Venetian who was captured at a young age and then taken to Tripoli, where he apostasized. From an initial position as a tax collector he rose meteorically by serving Uchalí (Alūj Ali) in Istanbul as official accountant and bursar, finally becoming king of Algiers in 1577 (Garcés 89).

31. A shawm was a medieval and Renaissance double-reed wind instrument similar to the modern oboe. Its penetrating sound was commonly employed in military or diplomatic settings, as here.

CADÍ.

Well then: has Spain made you rich? For it often does well by the
daring corsair.

YZUF.

My village was sacked. We found profit, though scant, and some
captives.

HAZÉN [*aside*].

You're more callous than Nero or the sacker of Sicily![32]

PASHA.

Bring some of them to me, and make sure they are the most
beautiful.

CAURALÍ.

I shall do it myself, sir, to please you.

[*Exit.*]

PASHA.

How many are there?

YZUF.

One hundred and twenty.

PASHA.

Are any of them fit for the galleys? Are there any skilled workers?

YZUF.

They are so good that the least of them will please you.

CADÍ.

Are there any young lads?

YZUF.

Only two; but of a rare beauty, as you'll soon see.

CADÍ.

Spain makes some beauties.

YZUF.

Well, you'll marvel at these. And I believe both are my nephews.

CADÍ.

You've done them a great favor.[33]

32. Hazén alludes here to Nero's role in burning Rome as well as to the Vandal Genseric or
Geiseric (389–477), a king who sacked Rome and Sicily (Cervantes 1998, 14:51).

33. Yzuf believes that captivity might improve his nephews' lives, as many janissaries were
captive boys raised to be soldiers.

HAZÉN [*aside*].

You did this, you traitor, you savage soul of Azzolino?[34]

[CAURALÍ *returns with the* OLD MAN, *who leads a child by the hand and carries a younger one in his arms, who does not speak; also the* SEXTON, DON FERNANDO, *and two other* CAPTIVES.]

CAURALÍ.

I believe this good old man is the father of those two boys.

YZUF.

I see my own face in his.

PASHA.

Was their mother taken captive?

CAURALÍ.

No, sir.

CADÍ.

This one is not bad looking.

PASHA.

They're very little.

CAURALÍ.

Despite that, in time I shall give two pageboys to Mohammed so they may serve him in their fashion, without their Rome hindering it.[35]

OLD MAN.

O wretch! What do I hear?

CADÍ.

Bring him over here.

OLD MAN.

Sir, don't separate us; I'm already struggling with fear, and it will conquer me.

CAURALÍ [*looking at* FERNANDO].

This is the desperate[36] man who threw himself into the sea after we'd set sail. A hook I cast caught him like a fish.

---

34. Azzolino da Romano (1194–1259) was an infamous Italian tyrant whom Dante places in the seventh circle of hell in the *Inferno*.

35. By "Rome" the Cadí refers to the boys' religion.

36. As noted above, "desperate" had connotations of suicide in early modern Spanish.

PASHA.

What moved him to do that?

CAURALÍ.

The love in his heart for a son he feared had come in our armada.

PASHA.

And the lad, what of him?

YZUF.

He's not here.

CADÍ.

How is that?

CAURALÍ.

He must have remained there.

FERNANDO.

Ah Costanza, what has become of you?

PASHA.

What are you saying?

FERNANDO.

Perhaps I lost her in the village!

PASHA.

It would have been better to look for her first, and if you could not find her, a ransom could have been supplied for her; it was a poor bargain to lose yourself for the sake of winning her. Who's this one?

CAURALÍ.

I'm not sure.

CAPTIVE.

Me, sir? I'm a carpenter.

HAZÉN [aside].

O unwise Christian! No money will see you safe from this storm. Skilled workers should not expect to escape while they live.[37]

CAURALÍ.

Should all the Christians come forth?

PASHA.

Just show me some of them.

---

37. Skilled workers—artisans, craftsmen, carpenters, masons, and the like—were highly valued and unlikely to be ransomed (Friedman 69).

[*Enter the* SEXTON.]

Is this one a priest?[38]

SEXTON.

I'm not a pope, only a poor sexton who can barely afford a cape.[39]

CADÍ.

What's your name?

SEXTON.

Tristán.

PASHA.

Your homeland?

SEXTON.

It's not on the map. It's Mollorido, a very remote village in Old
Castile. [*Aside.*] How this dog irks me! Heaven keep my senses
about me!

PASHA.

What is your trade?

SEXTON.

Playing, for I'm a divine musician, as you'll see.

HAZÉN.

Either this poor man's crazy or he's a buffoon.

PASHA.

Do you play the flute or shawm, or can you sing?

SEXTON.

I'm a sexton, so I play *ding, dong* at any time of day.

CADÍ.

Aren't those what you Christians call bells?

SEXTON.

Yes, sir.

PASHA.

You speak well: yours is divine music to us. Do you know how
to row?

38. The Spanish has *pápaz*, a word North African Muslims used to refer to Spanish clerics.
39. The Sexton puns on the Spanish *papa* (pope) and *capa* (cape); as Sevilla Arroyo and Rey
Hazas note, he may also be referring to the phrase *El papa y el que no tiene capa* (The pope and one
without a cape), which alludes to the power of death over all humankind (Cervantes 1998 14:54).

SEXTON.

No, my lord, for I'm afraid I'd burst; I'm in broken health.

CADÍ.

You'll watch the herds.

SEXTON.

I feel the cold in winter, and in summer I get so hot I can't even
speak.

PASHA.

This Christian is a buffoon.

SEXTON.

Me, a buffalo? No, sir; I'm a poor villager instead. What I'd be good
at would be guarding a door or fishing with a pole.

CADÍ.

Pick your trades well; you don't seem Spanish.

[*A* MOOR *enters.*]

MOOR.

The janissaries[40] await you in the palace.

PASHA.

Let us go. Farewell, captain! We shall see each other by and by.

CAURALÍ [*aside*].

Things are going my way! I've hidden the Christian woman; now
Fortune clears the path for me.

[*Exeunt all but* HAZÉN *and* YZUF.]

YZUF.

Now I'll speak to Hazén.

HAZÉN.

I want to speak with you. Let Cauralí leave so he can take the
captives, and let us stay here.

YZUF.

Be brief, for I have things to do.

HAZÉN.

So be it. I won't mention the fact that your soul keeps no law, neither

---

40. Janissaries were often recruited from Christian captives (cf. Yzuf's hopes for his nephews), as a contemporary source attests (Haedo 60). The janissary corps were well disciplined
and held privileged positions within the Ottoman army.

the letter nor the spirit, nor do you commend yourself to God in any church or mosque. Yet despite all this, I could never imagine cruelty so rare as to ignore the law of nature. If you obeyed it, you'd easily recognize the evil that you committed when you set foot on Spanish shores. What aggrieved Falaris, what enraged Dionysus, or what angry Catiline has ever vented his overwhelming cruelty on his own flesh and blood?[41] You raise your sword against your own homeland? Your sharp scythe cuts down the shoots that grew from your own blood?

YZUF.

My God, Hazén, you horrify me!

HAZÉN.

You are not horrified at having sold your uncle and your nephews, and your land, you unbeliever, and yet you're horrified . . .

YZUF.

You're speaking nonsense, you false Hazén. You must be a Christian.

HAZÉN.

You're right; and this hand will confirm it, forever ending your tyrannical behavior. [*He stabs* YZUF.]

YZUF.

Aaah, you've killed me! Mohammed, take vengeance now, as is your way!

HAZÉN.

You take high hopes to the lakes of Sodom![42]

[*The* CADÍ *returns.*]

CADÍ.

What's this? What shouts did I hear?

HAZÉN.

My God, the Cadí's coming back!

YZUF.

O sir, Hazén has slain me, and he is a Christian!

41. Falaris and Dionysus are examples of famous tyrants; Catiline, addressed in Cicero's *Catiline Orations*, conspired to overthrow the Roman government.

42. Lakes of Sodom: a reference to God's destruction of Sodom and Gomorrah in Genesis 19 for the cities' wickedness. They are often associated with homosexuality.

HAZÉN.

That's true: I'm a Christian, as you see me.

CADÍ.

Why did you kill him, dog?

HAZÉN.

I banish him from life not because he was a hunting dog but because his breed always erred in hunting.

CADÍ.

Are you a Christian?

HAZÉN.

Yes, I am, and so firm a Christian that, as you can see, I seek my own end to be with Christ, today if possible. O Lord, forgive my lack of faith, for, at the end of the day, if I denied you publicly, I now affirm you publicly! I know that this is what I must do as one who has offended you.

CADÍ.

Who ever saw such a thing? Stop, put him to death! Impale him now!⁴³

HAZÉN.

While I yet have this wood, with which I gratify my soul, yours will be a bed to lie on, Sardanapalus.⁴⁴ O my enemy, give me that bed, which my soul longs for; although it be hard on the body, give it to me, for heaven calls me to a great reward for it. [*He takes out a wooden cross.*] Don't change his mind, sweet Jesus; confirm his intent and my plea, for in the Cadí's cruelty lies my salvation.

CADÍ.

Walk! Carry him quickly and impale him on the shore.

HAZÉN.

This pole will get me the *palio*,⁴⁵ and thus I hasten.

---

43. Impalement was a torturous method of execution commonly depicted in European accounts of Barbary captivity. It involved piercing the victim's body with a stake and letting him hang on it until he died (Garcés 207).

44. A reference to the possibly fictitious last Assyrian king, said to have effete customs and a sensual, licentious lifestyle.

45. Hazén puns on the two senses of *palio* as a prize and as a clerical garment (*pallium*).

MOOR.

Move, you dog, move!

HAZÉN.

Christians, I go to my death not as a Moor but as a Christian; this can count against the low and profane life I've lived until today. Tell my parents in Spain, if you find yourselves freed from this exile.

CADÍ.

Cut off this dog's tongue! Finish him off! What are you doing? You carry this one away [*looking at* YZUF], and see if he's already breathed his last.

MOOR.

I think he's still breathing.

CADÍ.

Bring him to my house to be healed. This affair amazes me: I have seen a novel attempt, truly new under the sun. But in a Spanish dog, it should not surprise me.

[*Exeunt omnes.*]

▨   END OF ACT I   ▨

[*Enter* HALIMA, *Caralí's wife, and Doña* COSTANZA.[1]]

HALIMA.

How are you, Christian?

COSTANZA.

I am well, my lady; for I am fortunate to be yours.

HALIMA.

Clearly she who belongs to herself is better off. There's no misfortune like not having freedom: I know it well, though I'm no slave.

COSTANZA.

I was just thinking that, my lady.

HALIMA.

You're wrong. I am oppressed simply by being tied to my husband.

COSTANZA.

A wise woman makes a harsh husband gentle.

HALIMA.

Are you married?

COSTANZA.

I might have been, had heaven willed it, but it did not.

HALIMA.

Your nobility rivals your discretion.

[*Enter* CAURALÍ *and* DON FERNANDO *dressed as a captive.*]

CAURALÍ.

She's extremely beautiful; but her severity matches her beauty. Now, Love, spark in this hard stone the fire that consumes me! I've told you this so you can throw yourself into procuring my pleasure.

FERNANDO.

I'm obliged to do that and more, good master. Show me the captive,

---

1. We have respected the characters' titles in the original Spanish in order to preserve the class divisions within Spanish society. Don Fernando and Doña Costanza, for example, are of a higher social class than the Sexton or the Old Man.

and although she live free of Love's great power, you will soon see her either loving or compassionate over your pain.

CAURALÍ.

See her there; and this is Halima, my wife and your mistress.

FERNANDO.

I swear she's a worthy jewel!

HALIMA.

Well, friend, what's new?

CAURALÍ.

More than one ache that pains me.

HALIMA.

Has the king taken his share?

CAURALÍ.

That would be no misfortune.

HALIMA.

Well then, what's wrong?

CAURALÍ.

Isn't it cruel to send me back to roving right away? Yet Allah will make things better. I present you with this slave, a worthy Christian.

FERNANDO [aside].

Do I reason, see, hear, and feel? Is it the strain or the fear? Do my eyes not see before them the rich and noble spoils for whom I hurled myself into the sea? Is this not she who was my soul, and the reward for its ordeals?

CAURALÍ.

Tell me, who are you talking to, Christian? Why do you not prostrate yourself and kiss Halima's hand?

FERNANDO.

In the face of inhuman pain, he who errs most does best. Give me your feet, my lady, and see your captive prostrate before them.

HALIMA [aside].

I take as a captive one who will be my master. Do you know this captive?

FERNANDO.

Not at all.

COSTANZA [*aside*].

You spoke truly; and if sorrow erases memories, may this unhappy one die, so that she may not live forgotten. But perhaps you're dissembling and gathering lies that you think will be useful.

CAURALÍ.

Why do you mumble to yourself instead of speaking out loud?

FERNANDO.

What is your name?

COSTANZA.

Me? Costanza.

FERNANDO.

Are you single or married?

COSTANZA.

I had hoped to be married.

FERNANDO.

And have you lost hope now?

COSTANZA.

I still have confidence, for while life still remains it's foolish to lose hope of good fortune.

FERNANDO.

Who was your father?

COSTANZA.

Who? One Diego de la Bastida.

FERNANDO.

Weren't you to be married to one Don Fernando whose last name was de Andrada?

COSTANZA.

So I was, but the lucky day never arrived, for thanks to the traitor Yzuf, my lord Caurolí brought here the final version of the draft I only held in my hopes.

FERNANDO.

My lady, treat her well, for she is a noblewoman.

HALIMA.

Provided she serves me properly, I won't treat her ill.

[*Enter* ZARA, *well dressed.*]

ZARA.

Hazén has been impaled.

HALIMA.

Lady Zara, what's this about? I didn't expect you so soon.

ZARA.

The bagnio was not to my liking, and I left disgusted by that sad case.

HALIMA.

What case?

ZARA.

Hazén killed Yzuf, and the Cadí sentenced him to impalement that instant. I saw him die so happily that I think he did not die at all. If his death were by any other means, I would have envied it.

CAURALÍ.

But didn't he die as a Moor?

ZARA.

They say he kept a custom among Christians, which is to die confessing to the Christ whom they adore. I watched him and wept among many others, for my heart is naturally merciful and humane; in short, a woman's heart.

CAURALÍ.

You stopped to watch such a sight?

ZARA.

I'm curious and reckless.[2]

CAURALÍ.

Will you be here this afternoon, Zara?

ZARA.

Yes, for I have to review some things with Halima.

CAURALÍ.

Not the soldiers?

ZARA.

Perhaps.

2. This phrase recalls the intercalated novella in *Don Quixote* called *El curioso impertinente* (The Man Who Was Recklessly Curious) (Cervantes 2005, part 1, 33–35).

CAURALÍ.

May Allah be with you.

ZARA.

May He guard you.

[*Exit* CAURALÍ.]

HALIMA.

Don't you leave, Christian.

CAURALÍ.

Stay here.

FERNANDO.

It's plain speaking here in Barbary.

COSTANZA.

O fortunate misfortune of mine!

HALIMA.

Why?

COSTANZA.

For I gain from it.

ZARA.

What do you gain?

COSTANZA.

The good I had lost, which I recovered with my patience for the ills
I've suffered.

ZARA.

You learn much from experience!

COSTANZA.

I've seen much, and learned more.

ZARA.

Are these Christians new?

HALIMA.

Look at their clean faces and soft hands.

FERNANDO.

I shall leave if you command it.

HALIMA.

Have no fear, no Moor would suspect a captive, or be jealous of a
Christian. Save those honest manners for your land.

FERNANDO.

I shall.

HALIMA.

There's no Moorish woman here who would stoop to betray a Moor with a man of another faith, even if she knew he was secretly a king. That is why they allow us to talk to our captives.

FERNANDO.

A trusting oversight!

ZARA.

Work and pain dull the force of lust, and our great fear of being punished for our faults holds us all back, for it seems to me that turbulent desires appear everywhere. Come here; tell me, Christian, in your land is there anyone who makes a promise and doesn't keep it?

FERNANDO.

Perhaps some villain.

ZARA.

Even if he gives his faith, his word, and his hand in secret?

FERNANDO.

Even if the only witnesses are the heavens, which often reveal the truth.

ZARA.

And are they this loyal to their enemies?

FERNANDO.

To everyone; for the promise of the noble or gentleman is a proven debt, and a well-born man pledges always to be true.

HALIMA.

What do you care about the good or bad dealings of these men, who are dogs after all?

ZARA [aside].

O Allah, grant that those you had me choose be noble!

HALIMA.

What did you say, Zara?

ZARA.

Nothing; leave me alone, if you wish, with this virtuous slave of yours.

HALIMA.

How fond you are of knowing everything!

ZARA.

Who does not like to know?

HALIMA.

You speak to her, and I shall do the same with my slave.

COSTANZA [*aside*].

In the end what I feared has come true. What if Barbary concludes what Spain began? There I began to lose, and here I must lose all; for it's easy to see that this private conversation comes from love.

ZARA.

What is your name, friend?

COSTANZA.

Costanza.

ZARA.

You must be weary of having no freedom?

COSTANZA.

Truth be told, something else wearies me more.

HALIMA.

The softness or wear of your hands shows us how rich or poor you are. Show me, show me; it's foolish to hide them, for if you're to be ransomed I shall treat you justly and leniently.

ZARA.

What do you see?

COSTANZA.

I see a strange absurdity.

FERNANDO.

Mistress, my master is the one who should verify this, although it makes me laugh that you believe at all in such false science; for there are poor layabouts in our country who are both elegant and averse to work.[3]

---

3. Spanish novels of the time chronicle an aversion to work among both the rich and the poor, particularly in order to keep up the appearance of wealth. Such is the case with the famous squire in the picaresque *Life of Lazarillo de Tormes*, who is forced to eat the bread his servant receives as charity. Nobles of the lower orders often suffered from poverty while refusing to work.

HALIMA.

These hands bear witness to who you are; don't put yourself down.

COSTANZA [*aside*].

Ah, gypsy trickster! My misfortune is clear in those lines you read. How slowly you withdraw them, my enemy!

ZARA.

What's wrong, Christian?

COSTANZA.

What could be wrong? Nothing.

ZARA.

Were you ever by chance in love in your country?

COSTANZA.

Here, too.

ZARA.

Here, you say? How so? Are you taken with a Moor?

COSTANZA.

No, with a renegade of little and perjured faith.

FERNANDO.

You've seen enough, my lady.

ZARA.

Yours is a folly that no Christian woman has ever hit upon. Moorish women often love Christians, but for a Christian woman to love a Moor? Never.

COSTANZA.

I renege on that behavior.

HALIMA.

Why are you so distressed? You're quite shy.

FERNANDO.

Rich or poor, soft or hard, mistress, I'm your captive, and I consider it my good fortune.

COSTANZA.

This is a living death!

ZARA.

You love him so, poor woman? Today you love, and you arrived yesterday? How love inflames your heart! But how can one who resists it so poorly criticize you? What I regret about this, friend, is that I hear you say a Moor troubles such a beautiful Christian.

COSTANZA.

Not a Moor but a Mooress.[4]

ZARA.

You're talking nonsense; don't speak about that, for it's madness and futile error.

COSTANZA.

Love is wondrously foolish.

ZARA.

Yours makes that clear.

HALIMA.

What are you two talking about?

ZARA.

This Christian is worthy and witty!

HALIMA.

Well, this one is no fool either!

COSTANZA [aside].

He is of perjured and worthless faith.

HALIMA.

Let us go inside, for you've already heard the bad news, and the sun is burning overhead.

FERNANDO.

O my jewel, gladly recovered![5]

COSTANZA.

O my lost fortune!

---

4. The Spanish text plays on *moro* (Moor) and *mora* (Mooress). We have translated terms such as "Christian" and "Moor" in a gender-neutral way except in cases, such as this, that require clarification.

5. This lament refers to the Spanish poet Garcilaso de la Vega's tenth sonnet ("O dulces prendas, por mi mal halladas"). Garcilaso (1501–1536), one of the first Spanish practitioners of Petrarchism, was one of Cervantes's preferred poets and a classic in his own time.

[Exeunt. Enter the OLD MAN, *father of the children, and the* SEXTON; *the* OLD MAN *dressed as a captive,*[6] *and the* SEXTON *with his same outfit and a barrel of water.]*

SEXTON.

All we can do is have patience and put our trust in God; for it's sheer stupidity to give up and die.

OLD MAN.

Your conscience has gone lax, and now you eat meat on forbidden days.

SEXTON.

What nonsense! I eat whatever my master gives me.

OLD MAN.

It will do you no good.

SEXTON.

There's no theology here!

OLD MAN.

Don't you remember, by chance, those Hebrew children in scripture?

SEXTON.

You must mean the Maccabees, who let themselves be sliced to pieces before eating pork.[7]

OLD MAN.

That's right.

SEXTON.

If you begin to preach as soon as you see me, by God, I'll have to slip away whenever I see you.

OLD MAN.

You're stumbling already? May heaven grant that you do not fall.

SEXTON.

No chance of that, for my faith is made of bronze.

---

6. The typical garment of the captive was the *gilecuelco*—a dark blue or sky blue collarless jacket that did not extend past the elbows.

7. Cf. 2 Maccabees 7:1–42 for this brutal dismemberment. The Sexton's analogy is particularly interesting since he is a Christian, one only too happy to take advantage of Jewish dietary law (see page 57 of our translation).

OLD MAN.

I fear that if something's afoot with a Moorish woman, you'll hand over such zeal.

SEXTON.

Now, haven't two already given me what another might not reject?

OLD MAN.

Such favors are costly for those who take them and those who give them.[8] But enough of this. Who's your master?

SEXTON.

Mamí, a capable janissary who's a soldier and dabají, honest, and a Turk by nationality.[9] A dabají is the head of a squadron or second lieutenant, and the office suits him well, for he's courageous; and he's such an excellent dog that he neither bites me nor barks. So I praise my ill fortune, for if I had to be a captive, a wretched slave, at least it brought me under the wing of a janissary, and a brave one. For there's no Turk or anyone else who touches a janissary's captive, even if provoked to great anger by his insolence.

OLD MAN.

More captivity and sorrows befell my two sons, to increase my grief. Preserve the chastity of those ermines, O chaste heavens! And if you see that Mohammedan lewdness rise to make them fall, take their lives from them before they can be defiled.

[*Enter two or three* YOUNG MOORS, *perhaps even taken from the street,*[10] *who must say no more than these words.*]

---

8. Relations between Muslim women and men of different religions carried the death penalty in Ottoman society. However, Muslim men were allowed to marry non-Muslim women, so long as they were people of the Book—that is, Jewish or Christian.

9. Here the Sexton differentiates between *turcos de nación*, "Turks by nationality" (literally, "Turks by nation"), and *turcos de profesión*, "professed Turks" (or "renegades"). The latter were born Christian but converted to Islam. For further discussion, see Garcés 34–37 and Fuchs 2001, 122–25. Mamí was also the pirate who captured Cervantes as he was returning from military service in Italy.

10. Cervantes's stage direction is intriguing: while he may be referring to slaves or captives taken from the streets of Madrid, his casualness reminds the reader that Moors are not marked by any physical difference.

FIRST YOUNG MOOR.

Christian lad, no ransom, no escape; Don Juan[11] no come, die here, dog, die here!

SEXTON.

O son of a whore, grandson of a great cuckold, nephew of a rogue, brother of a great traitor and sodomite!

SECOND YOUNG MOOR.

No ransom, no escape, Don Juan no come, die here!

SEXTON.

You will die, you sot, you lying bugger; you don't play with a full deck, you're the bait of Mohammed, that whoreson!

THIRD YOUNG MOOR.

Die here!

OLD MAN.

Don't mention Mohammed, cursed be my lineage! They'll burn us alive.

SEXTON.

Let me deal with these dogs, even if I regret it later.

SECOND YOUNG MOOR.

Don Juan no come; die here!

OLD MAN.

If he had come, your cursed tongue would have no chance to say that.

FIRST YOUNG MOOR.

Don Juan no come; die here!

SEXTON.

Listen to me, puppies; come here, come here, hear me out, for I want to tell you why Don Juan doesn't come: pay attention. There must have been a great war in heaven where they were missing a general, and they took Don Juan for the job. Let him finish with that, and you'll see how he comes back and makes you as good as new.

---

11. Don Juan de Austria (1547–1578), the illegitimate son of the Holy Roman Emperor Charles I (V of Spain), commanded the Holy Alliance's triumphant naval forces at the battle of Lepanto (1571), during which Cervantes was wounded. Cervantes heaped praise on his former commander in several works.

OLD MAN.

A fine yarn! Now they've left.

[*Enter a* JEW.]

Isn't this one a Jew?

SEXTON.

His tuft gives him away, his wretched slippers, his mean and lowly
face.[12] Turks wear only one lock of hair combed up on their head,
and Jews wear it over their foreheads; the French, behind their ears;
and the Spaniards, stubborn as mules, mock everyone and wear
their hair—God help me!— all over their bodies. Hey, Jew! Listen.

JEW.

What do you want from me, Christian?

SEXTON.

I want you to lift this barrel and carry it to my master's house.

JEW.

It's the Sabbath, and I cannot perform any labor; I won't carry it,
even if you kill me. Let me come tomorrow, for even though it's
Sunday, I'll carry two hundred for you.

SEXTON.

Tomorrow I rest, Jewish dog. Load up, and let's not argue.

JEW.

Even if you kill me, I say I won't carry it.

SEXTON.

By God, you dog, I'll rip out your liver!

JEW.

Ah, ah, woe is me! By G-d almighty, if it weren't Saturday I'd carry
it! Enough, good Christian!

OLD MAN.

He moves me to compassion. O effeminate people, vile and worthless! For this one time I ask you to let him be.

---

12. After the expulsion of Spanish Jews in 1492, cultural production in Spain displayed a
marked prejudice and stereotypical image of Jews, who were identified mainly by their dress
and distaste for pork.

SEXTON.

I'll leave him for your sake. Let the vile circumcised one go; but if I find him again, he'll have to carry a mountain, if I've got one.

JEW.

I kiss your hands and feet, sir, and may G-d repay the good you've done me here.

[*Exits.*]

OLD MAN [*to the* JEW].

This is the punishment for that great sin. He who has already come, and whom you, in your error, vainly await, cast the eternal curse here fulfilled to the letter.[13]

SEXTON.

Farewell, for I've been talking to you a long time, and though my master is noble, I fear my laziness will make him mean.

[*He takes his barrel and exits. Enter* JUANICO *and* FRANCISCO,
for those are the names of the OLD MAN'S *sons; they are dressed
in the Turkish fashion as garzons,*[14] *and with them enter
Lady* CATALINA, *dressed as a garzon, and a* CHRISTIAN,
dressed as a captive, COSTANZA *and* DON FERNANDO,
as a captive, and JULIO, AS A CAPTIVE, *carrying the capes
and costumes of the garzons, and guitars and a rebec;*[15]
DON FERNANDO *should lead the way.*]

OLD MAN.

Are these not my jewels? Why are they dressed for revelry and celebrations? My happily found treasures, what finery is this? These are very expensive clothes. What happened to the clothing that showed in a thousand ways that, though poor, you were Christ's sheep?

13. The "great sin" here is the Jews' perceived responsibility for the Crucifixion of Christ, whom Christians believe to be the true Messiah. Moreover, the "eternal curse" refers to the story of the Wandering Jew, who taunted Christ at the Crucifixion and was condemned to wander the earth until the Second Coming, as Sevilla Arroyo and Rey Hazas note (Cervantes 1998, 14:77).

14. *Garzon,* from the French *garçon,* may designate a catamite (a boy kept for homosexual use) in early modern Spanish, especially when referring to the Ottomans or North Africa. Not all sources agree on this definition, however, and Covarrubias does not mention homosexuality.

15. A medieval string instrument played with a bow (*OED,* s.v. *rebec*); it was associated with pastoral life and song in Spain.

JUANICO.

Father, don't cry over our change of clothes, there was no way
around it; and, if you think about it, there's nothing to worry about,
for if our love of God stands firm, everyone knows clothes can't
undo what the heart does.

FRANCISCO.

Father, do you by chance have something for me to eat?

OLD MAN.

Was there ever so foolish a creature?

JUANICO.

Foolish? Just let him be, and he'll show you his prudence.

JULIO.

Friend, don't hold us back; and come with us if you like.

JUANICO.

No, sir; it would be better for him to stay.

FRANCISCO.

Father, here, put this cross they've taken from me in my rosary.[16]

OLD MAN.

I'll gladly do it for you, storehouse and reliquary of my soul.

JUANICO.

Good father, let us go, for we tarry.

[AMBROSIO, *who is Lady* CATALINA]

AMBROSIO.

Where are we headed, friends?

JULIO.

To Agimorato's garden,[17] though it's a ways from here.

FERNANDO.

Well, come then—let's not delay.

JULIO.

There we can dance, caper about, sing and play our instruments

---

16. Both Muslim and Christian believers employ prayer beads, as seen in the exchange between Lope and Vivanco in Act I. In Islam, the *Subḥa* or *misbaha* is used to recite the ninety-nine
names of Allah (*Encyclopedia of Islam*, s.v. "Subḥa"). There is another discussion of beads involving Zara, Costanza, and Halima in Act III. In all cases, Cervantes plays with the similarities between Christian and Muslim rosaries.

17. Agimorato plays a crucial role in the captive's tale in *Don Quixote*, part 1 (chapters 39–41).
Cf. Act 1, note 23.

undisturbed: for the sea is not always rough. Let us give our cares a rest, especially as the Cadí wants us to take our ease and enjoy honest sport on Fridays.

FERNANDO.

Who told you that I had a good voice?

JULIO.

I don't know, by my faith; it must have been some captive, and the Cadí told me: "Go, and tell Cauralí from me to send over his tallest Christian, the one with the good voice." I went, I spoke to him, and he sent you here; I don't know the rest.

JUANICO.

Don't disobey to come see us, father, for our master will become angry and let us know it.

FRANCISCO.

Father, my name is Francisco, not Hassan, Ali, or Jaer; I'm a Christian and shall remain one even with two garrotes and a knife to my neck.

JUANICO.

You see he knows how to say it? And he'll do it even better.

FERNANDO.

Let us go no farther, for we're fine here.

JULIO.

So be it; sing something.

[AMBROSIO, *who must by played by Lady* CATALINA]

AMBROSIO.

What did you say? I didn't hear you.

JULIO.

Chant, so I may be enchanted.

FERNANDO.

Is he deaf?

JULIO.

He's a little hard of hearing.

AMBROSIO.

Is there anyone who might hear us? Then it's a good idea, and since you've all come, let us begin sadly. We'll sing that ballad that you wrote, Julio, for we know it by heart, and it has that sad tone that cheers us.

[*They sing this ballad.*]

On the shores of the sea,
Whose bay and waters
Reach the walls of that infidel Algiers
Now turbulent, now calm;
Four wretched captives,
Resting from their labors,
With eyes of longing
Look to their homeland,
And to the tone of the ebb and flow
Of the waves on the shore,
In faint voices they sing and lament:
How dear you are to attain, o sweet Spain!
The heavens above have conspired
With our unlucky fate:
Our souls are in great danger,
And our bodies are in chains;
Oh if only the heavens would open
Their sealed watery gates
And instead of rain let fall here
Pitch and resin, sulfur and flames!
Oh if only the earth would open
To hide in its entrails
So many Datans and Abirams,[18]
So many sorcerers and witches!
How dear you are to attain, o sweet Spain!

FRANCISCO.

Father, have them sing that song my mother sang in our village. How does it go? Don't you want to, father?

---

18. In Numbers 16, Datan and Abiram, along with Korah, rebelled against Moses and Aaron and were swallowed up by the earth as a consequence. There is no link, however, between them and witchcraft.

OLD MAN.

How did the song go?

FRANCISCO.

I am in love,
With whom I won't say;
Eyes look where they love,
Where they love full well.

OLD MAN.

The song is fitting, since the eyes of the soul gaze from this cursed shore to the homeland for which they sigh, which retreats and awaits us not.

JULIO.

Francisquito is excellent! Now you sing, Ambrosio, a bit of what you usually sing alone, for the waves of the sea will hear you with infinite pleasure.

[AMBROSIO *sings alone.*]

Although you think I'm happy,
I carry my pain inside.
Although my face shows
Grief leaving my soul
And setting it free, know
That it's a clear mistake:
I carry my pain inside.
I must pretend
So I can end my end,
And because silent woes
Grow apace,
I carry my pain inside.[19]

[*Enter the* CADÍ *and* CAURALÍ.]

JUANICO.

That's enough; the Cadí's coming. Father, don't let him find you here.

FERNANDO.

Cauralí's with him.

---

19. Both songs the captives sing are traditional ballads.

OLD MAN.

Farewell, beloved jewels!

CADÍ.

You here, dog? Haven't I told you to stop trying to see your sons, you scoundrel?

FRANCISCO.

Why? Is he not my father? By my faith, I must see him in spite of you!

JUANICO.

Quiet, Francisquito, my brother, for what you say makes this tyrant want to harm us.

FRANCISCO.

You won't allow us to see our father? You're never a good Christian. Father, take me with you, for this my enemy tells me so many lies.

CAURALÍ.

What clever trifles! Tell me,
what are you waiting for, friend?

[*Exit the* OLD MAN.]

CADÍ.

Dog, if you allow that mongrel to speak to them again, you'll see what you get for it.

JULIO.

They're pieces of his soul.

CADÍ.

What did you say to me, you dog?

CAURALÍ.

Be still, he didn't say anything.

FRANCISCO.

My goodness, the fine Moorish lady is so upset!

JUANICO.

Quiet, brother, on your life!

CAURALÍ.

He's very witty.

CADÍ.

Don't you think? I adore him, and I intend to adopt him after making him a Moor.

FRANCISCO.

Well, know that I'll make fun of you even if you give me mountains of gold; and even if you give me three right, proper, and complete reales, and two maravedís more.[20]

CADÍ.

What do you think of these graces?

CAURALÍ.

They're supernatural.

CADÍ.

Follow me into the city.

CAURALÍ.

I want to speak with my slave.

CADÍ.

Well then, may Allah be with you.

CAURALÍ.

And also with you. [*To Fernando:*] You know already of my great need.

[*The* CADÍ *exits with everyone but* DON FERNANDO *and* CAURALÍ.]

FERNANDO.

I'll speak to her on my way home, and do whatever I can to serve you, though she prove harder than a mountain or more terrible than an asp. Just let me speak to her and I'll get to work, master.

CAURALÍ.

If you conquer her, you shall have the victor's prize in battle.

FERNANDO.

I believe it.

CAURALÍ.

I mean that in addition to a lot of money, I'll give you your freedom.

FERNANDO.

I expect even more mercies from your generosity.

[*Exeunt. Enter* DON LOPE *and* VIVANCO.]

LOPE.

Here we are, freed by the strangest case captivity has ever seen.

---

20. See the Introduction for a fuller discussion of these coins.

VIVANCO.

Do you think this has been by chance? It's truly mysterious! God, who wants this Moor to journey to a land that adores His name, moved her to become the instrument that improved all our fortunes.

LOPE.

In her last note, she said that on Friday she'll take the gate of Bab-al-Wad to the countryside,[21] and that she promises to show herself by a certain ruse. She ended by saying that we must seek out her father Agimorato's garden, where our dealings and our act will come to their happy ending.[22]

VIVANCO.

She has given us three thousand escudos in all.

LOPE.

Buying our freedom cost us two thousand.

VIVANCO.

We've gained far more than what we've lost. And even more, perhaps, if we win this soul, who is Christian in deeds even if moored in a Moorish body. But wait, what if this is the woman?

LOPE.

If it is, she's beautiful, by my faith!

[*Enter* ZARA *and* HALIMA, *their faces covered with white mantles; and with them, dressed as Moors,* COSTANZA *and Lady* CATALINA, *who speaks but two or three times.*]

LOPE.

But which of the two is she? The others are captives.

HALIMA.

All the same, I know that if you speak to him . . .

COSTANZA.

Don't lose hope, for God's sake. I volunteer to speak to him and to persuade and compel him so that he comes to adore you; but you must give me a chance to talk to him.

---

21. Bab-al-Wad (*Vavalvete* in the Spanish) was one of the nine gates of Algiers (Haedo 31).

22. In one of the more metatheatrical moments of the play, Lope puns on an earlier version of this story, a play Cervantes entitled *El trato de Argel* (The Traffic of Algiers).

HALIMA.

You shall have whatever you want, my friend; don't let that stop you from helping me in my hardship.

ZARA.

Walk, Halima, if you can.

COSTANZA.

I am bound by your goodness to do even more than that.

ZARA.

Look at those two, Costanza, and see if by chance you know either of them.

COSTANZA.

I don't know either one.

VIVANCO.

If it is her, we are fortunate, for her vivacity makes her extremely beautiful.

ZARA.

They are dashing pups! Oh, that I might speak to them!

HALIMA.

If mine were there, I would go speak to them.

ZARA.

Costanza, look at them again, and tell me if you can tell whether they seem noble.

CATALINA.

Why?

ZARA.

So I can buy them.

COSTANZA.

The one on the left looks like a gentleman, and even the other is no peasant.

ZARA.

I want to see them up close.

HALIMA.

If only my Christian were here!

ZARA.

Both of them satisfy me.

VIVANCO.

How they hesitate! Let's go over there.

LOPE.

No, they're coming over here.

VIVANCO.

Their vivacity and appearance are pleasing.

ZARA.

Oh, Allah! What stung me? Look around, Costanza, and see if
there's a wasp. Woe is me, for it seems that a lance has pierced
my neck. Shake this veil out, for I'm going mad at what I see. Ah,
unlucky me! Did you kill it? Didn't you see it? Shake my veil again;
look and feel around. What if it's still there!

COSTANZA.

I don't see anything.

ZARA.

This unseen sting has gone to my heart!

COSTANZA.

The sting of the wasp inflames greatly; but I'm worried it might be a
spider.

ZARA.

If it was a spider, it was Spanish; for the Algerian ones do no harm.

LOPE.

Have you ever seen such a ruse? Was there ever such a clever trick?

HALIMA.

Zara, don't look so disheveled; put your veil back on.

ZARA.

Even the air bothers me.

HALIMA.

This misfortune, though slight, has ruined our jaunt.

VIVANCO.

What do you think?

LOPE.

I think my good fortune offers me everything I could want.

VIVANCO.

The sun is hidden again; its light is gone.

ZARA.

Could you, Costanza, ask that captive if he is Spanish?

COSTANZA.

I would be pleased to do so.

LOPE.

Show yourself again, oh sun! whose rays light my being, my understanding, my good fortune and happiness in having you.

ZARA.

Ask him, Costanza.

HALIMA.

How are you?

ZARA.

I feel better.

COSTANZA.

Sir, are you from Spain?

LOPE.

Yes, my lady; and from a land that does not breed poisonous spiders—a land with no fraud, tricks, or ruses but instead honest dealing, where promising and keeping promises are one and the same thing.

ZARA.

Ask him if his wife is pretty, if he's married.

COSTANZA.

Are you married?

LOPE.

No, my lady; but I shall be quite soon to a Christian Moor.

COSTANZA.

How can that be?

LOPE.

How can that be? If you don't know, you're ill informed. She who will be my mistress is a Moor by her incredulity, and a Christian by her kindness.

COSTANZA.

I'm too thick to make out what you're saying.

ZARA.

May it please Allah that you speak truly!

HALIMA.

Ask him if he is a slave or a freeman.

LOPE.

Now I understand you; I pride myself on being a captive.

ZARA.

I understand all he says, and I know what he means.

LOPE.

I shall soon set foot on Spanish shores with pleasure and rare glory, and then I'll show my firm faith.

ZARA.

Thanks to Allah and a pole.

HALIMA.

Christians, stay back, for we're entering the city.

[*The Moorish ladies exit.*]

VIVANCO.

We shall obey you.

LOPE.

We are left in darkness. Beautiful sun, why do you go? Your generosity freed the body that you rescued from captivity; but your beauty has bound my soul in irons. From what I've seen in you, and of the desire that rules over you, I cannot keep from adoring you, as a jewel not of Mohammed but of Christ. I shall take you where you can be everything that you desire, even if it costs me a thousand lives.

VIVANCO.

Let's go, this is our sorrow; not that way, you're wandering.

[*Exeunt. Enter the* SEXTON *with a pot of mojí stew,*²³ *and the* JEW *after him.*]

JEW.

Honorable Christian, may G-d return you to your freedom, just as you return what is mine.

SEXTON.

I don't want to, honorable Jew; honorable Jew, I don't want to.

---

23. This type of casserole was made with breadcrumbs, honey, cheese, and eggplant (*Diccionario de Autoridades*), and was perceived to be typical of Jewish cuisine. It appears in the list of dishes favored by the *conversa* Aldonza in Delicado's *La Lozana Andaluza* (Mamotreto [Chapter] II).

JEW.

Today is Saturday, and I have nothing to eat, so I feed myself with what I cooked yesterday.

SEXTON.

Cook something else.

JEW.

No, for I'd go against my law.

SEXTON.

Ransom this pot from me, and in giving it to you I shall do no small thing, for its smell consoles me.

JEW.

I can't deal in large or in small sums.

SEXTON.

Well then, I'll take it.

JEW.

Don't take it. This is what it cost.

SEXTON.

So be it, for this benefits us both. Where's the money?

JEW.

Here, I have it in my shirt, woe is me!

SEXTON.

Well then, let's have it.

JEW.

You take it, for my law doesn't allow me to.

SEXTON.

Beelzebub take you if he can, you seed of Habbakuk![24] Here you have exactly fifteen silver reales.

JEW.

Don't bargain with me; deal with yourself.

SEXTON.

Tell me, pot: What are you worth? "I think I'm worth five reales, and no more." You lie, by my faith as a gentleman!

JEW.

What a fright you're giving me, Christian!

---

24. For another reference to Habbakuk, see Act I (page 13 of our translation).

SEXTON.

Wait, let the dog speak. You don't want to go on? Here, I want to give you credit: take it, and go with God.

JEW.

And the other ten?

SEXTON.

That's for two other stews I plan to steal from you.

JEW.

And you paid in advance?

SEXTON.

And if I tally up carefully, I think I've even been cheated.

JEW.

Is there a heaven that allows such things?

SEXTON.

Is there such a delicious dish? It's not nerve meat or meat that sticks to the ribs of the bay horse, which is *tref*.[25]

JEW.

Heaven grant that this petty thief leave me alone!

SEXTON.

Petty thief? By God, I shall rob a child from you before two months are up; and even if I season its feet . . . God knows what I mean! Let's go!

> [*Exeunt. Enter* DON FERNANDO *and* COSTANZA.]

FERNANDO.

I climbed, as I said, that cliff, where I saw the galleys setting sail. I began to shout; but no one answered, although they all heard me well enough. Echo, who hides herself in a crag there, where the waves break furiously, took pity on my suffering and gave an answer to my last words. I renewed my cries; I signaled with my arm and my handkerchief; Echo came back, and from the same cliffs repeated my bitter words. Is there any remedy to the pain you cause, Love, that you cannot teach? You taught me one, such that I found life where I sought death. My heart, which let its pain out

---

25. In this passage the Sexton employs the word *trefe*, from the Hebrew *t'ref*, "forbidden meat, impure food."

through my eyes in rivers of tears (that humor that makes embers seem to burn more brightly in the amorous forge), made me hurl myself into the sea with no thought of dangers or obstacles, convinced that to be reunited with its soul would be a worthy prize. Flinging away my weapons, I flung myself into the sea, burning in amorous fire, and became another Leander,[26] with more light, for I was following yours. My arms grew tired, and I made a great effort, bursting past death and through the sea, for I saw that a galley was coming back for me, for its profit and my good fortune. A Turk cast out a curved iron and hooked me, like useless bait, and with great effort finally raised me onto the enemy boat, and I don't know what else to tell you of my story. Cauralí made me one of his own; his wife, my enemy, chases after me, and he chases after you. Behold a story worthy of amazement and compassion!

COSTANZA.

If you remain firm in the face of Halima's pleas, as I hope, I shall be tough as steel to Cauralí's file, impenetrable and worthy. But we'll have to give them some sign of amorous feeling so that they let us see each other and relieve our suffering. Cauralí begged you to speak to me, and Halima asked me to speak to you.

FERNANDO.

Something troubles me more than his suffering.

COSTANZA.

And me.

FERNANDO.

May these embraces break their plans to pieces; so long as we manage this, we should not fear any worry or peril, for I have heaven in my arms.

[*Enter* CAURALÍ *and* HALIMA, *and they see them embracing.*]
Hold me tight, dear wife, for so long as my anguished soul rests in this heaven, harsh Fortune can bring me no evil on earth.

---

26. Cervantes again quotes from Garcilaso's work, this time from a sonnet dedicated to Hero and Leander. The tragic story tells of two lovers separated by the Hellespont.

CAURALÍ.

Dog! You, with my slave? How is it that heaven does not smite you?

HALIMA.

Bitch! You, with my captive? How can I refrain from killing you? This is what I expected, bitch!

CAURALÍ.

Dog!

HALIMA.

Bitch!

CAURALÍ.

Dog!

HALIMA.

The fault lies with this bitch; your captive did not come up with the wrongdoing.

CAURALÍ.

He did come up with it, really, and I'm sure I'm not wrong.

[*To* FERNANDO:] I'll rip out your heart, you dog!

HALIMA [*to* COSTANZA].

Bitch, you'll pay with your life for this treachery!

FERNANDO.

Oh, how you misunderstand our intention, my masters! That embrace you saw, Costanza was sending it to you.

CAURALÍ.

What are you saying?

FERNANDO [*aside*].

What you heard, you wretch.

COSTANZA.

The favor you interrupted was carried out in your name. Truly, you're choleric!

FERNANDO.

Understand this and believe it.

HALIMA.

What do you say, my friend?

COSTANZA.

If this embrace was lost, tomorrow I'll collect four more.

CAURALÍ.

Is what you have said true?

FERNANDO.

Well, why would I lie to you?

CAURALÍ.

Be certain of your liberty.

HALIMA.

I could scold you more for this love or immodesty; but I shall leave off until I see whether you keep doing what I've seen and can't believe.

CAURALÍ.

Halima, in a thousand ways I confirm that you're a prudent woman, especially given that these two, as new Christians, must just have paid tribute to their pleasure, since captives and countrymen are filled with joy at seeing each other, and as they found themselves alone, they shared their sorrows.

HALIMA.

And even those of others.

CAURALÍ.

This doesn't seem right to me.

COSTANZA.

Both of them figured it out.

CAURALÍ.

Does Halima happen to know anything about this?

HALIMA.

Is Cauralí by chance pining for your love?

COSTANZA.

That's madness!

FERNANDO.

Let no such worry weigh on you, for she hasn't figured it out.

COSTANZA.

My lady, be satisfied and suspect no harm.

CAURALÍ.

One can easily be tricked.

COSTANZA.

And dishonor shows up at the eleventh hour.[27]

CAURALÍ.

Do whatever you can and know how to do.

HALIMA.

Don't let your guard down at all.

CAURALÍ.

It's good that your rage is over.

HALIMA.

Think of it as past. Go and find me those keys.

[*Exit* HALIMA *and* COSTANZA.]

CAURALÍ.

You, see me to the Zoco.[28]

FERNANDO.

Love, though I follow you heart and soul; I now bless, now curse,
your scheming and straits.

[*Exeunt. Enter* JUANICO *and* FRANCISQUITO, *playing
with a spinning top.*]

FRANCISQUITO.

You, who pester me because I cut short your virtuous sobs, have you
ever seen a prettier top, God willing?

JUANICO.

Stop throwing those nooses, for heavier ones await our throats.

FRANCISQUITO.

You're scared of that, brother? I'll break them into a million pieces.
Don't think that I'll become a Moor, even if this monster promises
me silver and gold, for I'm a Spanish Christian.

JUANICO.

That's what I'm afraid of, and why I cry.

FRANCISQUITO.

Because I'm young, you don't believe in my courage.

---

27. All editions of the text have Costanza speak this line, though it would make more sense
for Halima to say it. We have respected the original in this case.

28. Zoco: the main thoroughfare in Algiers.

JUANICO.

That's right.

FRANCISQUITO.

Well, know that I have divine strength to resist human tyranny. I don't know who counsels me with a quiet voice in my heart (for I don't hear it in my ear) and leaves me pleased and content to die; they tell me that I shall be a new Justus, and you a new Pastor, which I like.[29]

JUANICO.

Make it so, divine love, for I bow to your will. Leave this childish top, on my life! and let us go over our prayers.

FRANCISQUITO.

The Hail Mary is enough for me.

JUANICO.

And the Our Father?

FRANCISQUITO.

Also.

JUANICO.

And the Credo?

FRANCISQUITO.

I know it by heart.

JUANICO.

And the Salve Regina?[30]

FRANCISQUITO.

Even if they give me two tops, I shall not be a Moor!

JUANICO.

What foolishness!

FRANCISQUITO.

Well then: Do you think I'm joking?

---

29. Saints Justus and Pastor were schoolboys and Christian martyrs who died together, aged nine and thirteen, in the Diocletian persecutions during the Roman occupation of Spain (303 C.E.). They are venerated as patrons of Alcalá de Henares, Cervantes's birthplace, and Madrid.

30. As noted above in reference to Zara, these four prayers were cornerstones of post-Tridentine Catholic catechisms.

JUANICO.

We're speaking of manly things, and you bring up the top?

FRANCISQUITO.

Should I be crying constantly? By my faith, brother, worry about yourself, and beware that Mohammed's tempest doesn't sink you; for inside this sheath lies a soul that thirsts for God; and neither the top, nor the whip, nor all the fountains of Algiers and its surroundings will slake my divine thirst, nor will it ever be slaked except in Him. And so I tell you, brother, that you should not take my childishness for a lack of courage, for deep inside me there is no place without God. Worry about yourself, and commend yourself to God in the coming assault; if not, I shall go out to the plaza to fight for both of us. I have the Hail Mary nailed in my heart, and it is the star that guides me through this sea of affliction to the port of happiness.[31]

JUANICO.

God speaks through you, so I'm not surprised to see you speak in such high style.

FRANCISQUITO.

Nothing will upset you if you look upon her.

JUANICO.

Woe to us, for here comes the stubborn Cadí! We must be strong.

FRANCISQUITO.

Rely on the Hail Mary; you'll see what strength it has.

[*Enter the* CADÍ *and* CARAHOJA, *the master of the one who lost his ears.*]

CADÍ.

Well, my sons, what are you doing?

JUANICO.

My brother is spinning his top, as you see, my lord.

CARAHOJA.

He's a child, and it's fitting for his age.

---

31. Commonly, the Virgin Mary was given the title Stella Maris (Star of the Sea), a guiding light for sailors.

CADÍ.

And you, what are you doing?

JUANICO.

I was praying.

CADÍ.

For whom?

JUANICO.

For myself, for I'm a sinner.

CADÍ.

All this is well and good. What were you praying?

JUANICO.

What I know, my lord.

FRANCISQUITO.

He answered well. He was saying the Hail Mary. [*He plays with the top.*]

CADÍ.

You can stop the spinning before me, Bairán.

FRANCISQUITO.

A great name they've given me!

CARAHOJA.

It's all child's play.

CADÍ.

I pity this lad. Stop being so stubborn, Bairán, or you will suffer for it. What do you say?

FRANCISQUITO.

Hail Mary.

CADÍ.

What do you answer?

FRANCISQUITO.

Full of grace.

CARAHOJA.

This older one teaches the younger one.

JUANICO.

I don't teach him anything, for he himself is capable.

FRANCISQUITO.

Oh, now would be the time to say Our Father!

JUANICO.

Since our parents on earth are missing, we must resort to heaven.
Where's our father being kept?

FRANCISQUITO.

I shall call him in good time.

JUANICO.

The war is starting.

FRANCISQUITO.

To make everything right, I want to say the last thing that my
mother taught me, which is good for dying.

CADÍ.

What will you say?

FRANCISQUITO.

I believe in God the Father.

CADÍ.

By Allah, I'm ready to kill him!

FRANCISQUITO.

You're upset already? Well, if that bothers you, what will happen
when you hear me say the Salve Regina? To confound you all the
more, I know all of the four prayers, and know full well they are
shields against your scimitars and your lewd thoughts.

CARAHOJA.

You can be free of this fear if you just raise a finger and say "Ilá,
ilalá."[32]

FRANCISQUITO.

That's not in the primer, I can't say it.

JUANICO.

Nor do I want to, you should add.

FRANCISQUITO.

I was about to say that.

---

32. These words begin the Muslim credo, the recitation of which is the only marker of
conversion. While Christianity was tolerated in the bagnios, certain groups, such as women
and young boys who would become candidates for the janissary corps, were often objects of
proselytism.

CADÍ.

This is a worthless exercise! Take this one, on my orders, and that
other one, for they must die.

[FRANCISQUITO *throws away the top and undresses.*]

FRANCISQUITO.

Come now! Enough of this top, and of this gross outfit, which makes
my soul beastly: he who dares walk this road should go lightly
dressed. Come now, brother, be a strong and a brave shepherd, for
this little sinner, redeemed by the grace of God, will follow behind!
Come now, ferocious tyrants, show your hands at the ready, and
your sharp scythes for cutting the edges of these throats and voices,
for in this rare effort to which tyranny brings all its rage, you shall
not get from my mouth anything but . . .

JUANICO.

What?

FRANCISQUITO.

A Hail Mary.

CARAHOJA.

Let's go inside, for pleasure will make them change their mind more
than the whip and pole.

CADÍ.

By a million signs I sense that my suit goes poorly; for the older one
is very quiet and shrewd. I shall blaspheme Mohammed himself if
he does not tame these lads!

FRANCISQUITO.

Don't you fear him?

JUANICO.

I fear him not.

■   END OF ACT II   ■

Act III

[*Enter the* WARDEN PASHA *and another* MOOR]

WARDEN.

I won't give up my share for ten escudos. Sit down, and don't let anyone in unless they pay two full ásperos.

MOOR.

On Christmas, as they call it, it came to twenty-five ducats.

WARDEN.

The Spaniards, for their part, are putting on a great play.[1]

MOOR.

They are Satans and very devils; they can do anything. Now they're off to their Mass.

[*Enter* VIVANCO, DON FERNANDO, DON LOPE, *the* SEXTON, *the* FATHER *of the children;* DON FERNANDO *carries the Sexton's breeches.*]

FERNANDO.

Here they are—I haven't put them on. Earlier, Costanza mended them where they needed it, with her own hands.

SEXTON.

They're perfect for the play; I'll put them on now. To it, let's go!

WARDEN.

Where are you going, Christian?

FATHER.

Me? To hear Mass.

MOOR.

Then pay.

FATHER.

What? Pay? One must pay here?

---

1. Because a captive slave's value diminished if he apostatized by renouncing Christianity and converting to Islam, religious tolerance was encouraged in the bagnios. Mass was said regularly, and on holy days there were celebrations such as processions and theater pieces; other slaves could pay to see the festivities. See Friedman 77–85.

WARDEN.

Clearly this old father is new here!

MOOR.

Two ásperos, or step aside, move on.

FATHER.

I don't have them, by God.

MOOR.

Then go hang yourself.

LOPE.

I'll pay for him.

MOOR.

That's fine.

SEXTON.

Effendi, let me in, and take this handkerchief that I stole from a Jew not half an hour ago as a token. Or give me what it's worth, for I'll give it to you at cost, or for just a little more.

WARDEN [*to the* MOOR].

With these four more you've done very well.

SEXTON.

Right, then, I'm going in.

MOOR.

Hurry inside, for it's getting late. With the king's captives, I bet there are more than two thousand in the bagnio. Let's watch from the door how they say their Mass, for I imagine in concert they must have excellent music.

WARDEN.

Stand behind the gate and you'll see everything the Christians do in the yard, for it's a sight to see.

MOOR.

I've already seen them. They say their Christ was reborn today.

[*Exeunt. Enter all of the* CHRISTIANS *there are, and* OSORIO *among them, and the* SEXTON, *wearing the breeches that* FERNANDO *gave him.*]

OSORIO.

This is a new mystery. Today twenty holy men have celebrated the Resurrection of Christ with a musical arrangement, which they call

counterpoint. Algiers, I suspect, is a small Noah's ark: here are men
of all kinds, trades, and skills, and of disguised ranks.[2]

VIVANCO.

There's another thing to marvel at even more, if you notice: as anyone can see, these faithless dogs allow us to practice our religion.
They let us say our Mass, though in secret.

OSORIO.

On more than one occasion it's been celebrated in haste and with
difficulty. Once they took the priest in his vestments from the altar
and dragged him through the village streets. They were so cruel to
him that he ended both life and liberty on the road. But let's forget
this talk and attend to our pleasure, since our masters give us the
chance. The first days of Easter are our own.

LOPE.

So what? Are there musicians here?

OSORIO.

And skillful ones; we'll call the Cadí's men.

VIVANCO.

Here they are.

OSORIO.

And the one who's helping with the piece is already here.

FERNANDO.

The Cadí's musicians sing well!

OSORIO.

Before more people arrive, let the dialogue begin, for it's by the great
Lope de Rueda, printed by Timoneda,[3] who defeats Time in his
old age. I couldn't find a shorter piece to perform, and I know it will
please with its strange rustic speech.

VIVANCO.

Do we have sheepskin jackets?

---

2. Skilled craftsmen, as noted above, were less likely to be ransomed and thus might "disguise their ranks."

3. Lope de Rueda (1505?–1565) was one of the founders of modern Spanish drama; Timoneda (1500–1583), a writer and bookseller, published Rueda's *pasos*, or skits. Cervantes may
have met Timoneda, thus the allusion to his old age. See Cervantes 1998, 14:108.

OSORIO.

Humble ones; I'm going to get dressed.

VIVANCO.

Who's singing?

OSORIO.

The Sexton here, who's full of graces.

VIVANCO.

Is there a prologue?

OSORIO.

By no means!

[*Exit* OSORIO *and the* SEXTON.]

VIVANCO.

Oh, how beggarly they look! Well, it's a captive play: poor, hungry, and unhappy, bare and clumsy.[4]

LOPE.

May its intention come across.

[*Enter* CAURALÍ.]

CAURALÍ.

Sit down; don't be alarmed, for I've come to see your celebration.

FERNANDO.

I wish it were worthy of you, Effendi.

LOPE.

You may sit here; I'll stand.

CAURALÍ.

No, no, friend, sit down; they're starting.

LOPE.

Here they come; hush, they're singing.

VIVANCO.

They should be crying.

FERNANDO.

This day allows no tears.

[*They sing whatever they like.*]

4. Cervantes plays here on the genre he himself invented: the *comedia de cautivos*, or captivity play.

VIVANCO.

The music was heretical; if the dialogue is like that, both rudder and axle will break before the wheel can turn.

[*When the music ends, the* SEXTON *speaks (all that the* SEXTON *now says, he says while looking at* CAURALÍ *out of the corner of his eye):*]

SEXTON.

What is this? What land is this? What do I hear? What do I see? This celebration is a requiem for me, for a more than deathly desire vexes me. Where was this fire lit, that amid jokes and games turns my soul to ash? This arrow is from Mohammed, whose force I deny. Like the sun, which, when it peers over a low mountain, takes us unawares and with its sight tames and disarms our sight; like the carbuncle, which resists all decay, so is your countenance, Aja, a hard lance of Mohammed that tears my entrails apart.[5]

CAURALÍ.

Is this part of the play, or is this Christian a jester?[6]

SEXTON.

If her shining white hand does not remedy my pain, all shall end in tragedy. O most beautiful Moor, the most intelligent and gracious one known to Fame, from where daybreak dawns to where the sun rests [*He says this looking at* CAURALÍ], may Mohammed keep you countless centuries in his company.

CAURALÍ.

Is this dog rambling, or is this part of the story for today's celebration?

FERNANDO.

Quiet, Tristán, and pay attention, for the dialogue is starting.

SEXTON.

I shall try, but I don't know if I'll be able to, the devil tempts me so.

---

5. The Sexton seems to be mocking Cauralí for his love of a Christian. Exogamous romance was a theme common to both Spanish and English drama of the period. These exact lines are repeated in *El amante liberal* (The Generous Lover), one of the stories in Cervantes's collection of *Novelas ejemplares* (Exemplary Novellas), which deals with exogamous romance.

6. Early modern Spanish plays would include interludes such as this, in which the Sexton makes fun of the various love plots. Cervantes here plays with the convention, as the Sexton is not scheduled to present an interlude during the colloquy. Colloquies were a traditional theatrical genre involving a dramatic conversation in dialogue form.

[*Enter* GUILLERMO, *shepherd.*]

GUILLERMO.

If the gladness I feel, which has come on so swiftly, doesn't fill out my pouch, what patches shall I place on my tunic, and how shall I let out my doublet?[7]

SEXTON.

By God, my liver's afire, and I suffer and keep quiet![8]

GUILLERMO.

If this goes on, it might be better to stop.

SEXTON.

Who lit this ember?

LOPE.

Tristán, friend, listen, for you are prudent, and hush, for this is very impertinent.

SEXTON.

I shall keep quiet and have patience.

GUILLERMO.

Shall I begin?

LOPE.

Yes, begin.

GUILLERMO.

If the gladness I feel, which has come on so suddenly, doesn't fill out my pouch, what patches shall I place on my tunic, and how shall I let out my doublet? And if, to tell it fully,[9] Costanza[10] happily looked upon me yesterday, what commotion or change might there be now that she doesn't even dream of me?

---

7. The colloquy this shepherd sings may have its source in one called *Gila*, published by Timoneda in 1567 (Cervantes 1998, 14:111).

8. According to the Galenic theory of humors, the liver was the source of black bile and thus when aggravated could produce melancholy, sadness, or, as here, lust.

9. The original has *al contarlo extremeño*, which could signify "happily" or "rustically." In the facsimile of the 1615 edition, the text reads *Extremeño*, which editors correct to a lower-case *e*. This word may be related to the Extremadura region's association with pastoral culture. Most likely, Cervantes is playing with the word *extremo* and changing it for rhyme, meaning something more like "fully."

10. In another metatheatrical moment, a beloved Costanza is referred to in the colloquy.

Spread out, my sheep, over meadows and fields; eat tasty bits, never
fear the coming night with its angry clouds; roam free, leaping with
glee. Don't worry about being eaten by starving she-wolves, greedy
and disgruntled; and, when it's time to give up your fleeces, come
easily instead of lazily, grazing on the hillsides, to nearby journey-
men or the snip of their scissors; for an infinite happiness, beyond
imagining, will free you from harm if you but suspect the gladness
I feel when you give up your white fleece. Yet who is the frightened
wretch who approaches in a daze, head down, hair and beard standing on end, bowed down and disheartened?

SEXTON.

Who should it be? I am the sad and unfortunate one, alive one
moment and dead the next, in love with Mohammed.

CAURALÍ.

Throw this madman out!

SEXTON.

I invoke your divine mouth, Aja, of a thousand orange blossoms,
mouth of consolations, which I touch from afar!

CAURALÍ.

Let me at him!

FERNANDO.

No, master, for everything he says is a joke. The sinner's a jester.

SEXTON.

God of the winds! Is there no breeze to temper such heat?

GUILLERMO.

This is too much insolence and foolishness! Throw him out already,
and leave us!

SEXTON.

I'm going. God be with you, my Algerian glory!

[*Exits.*]

GUILLERMO.

Where was I?

VIVANCO.

I don't know.

LOPE.

"Yet, who is the frightened wretch ... ?" was the line at which he stopped.

FERNANDO.

The breeches worked.

GUILLERMO.

Should I start again?

FERNANDO.

No, no; don't let them disturb us at a bad time. Continue the dialogue.

[*A* MOOR *says from above:*]

MOOR.

Christians, be alert; close the gate to the bagnio!

GUILLERMO.

Cursed be the hour in which you came, you dog!

MORO.

Open up for this Christian, who is hurt, and close straightaway!

CAURALÍ.

Allah help me! What is this?

MOOR.

O holy Allah almighty! They have killed two of the king's captives. Oh unheard of cruelty! They are killing everyone without distinction.

[*Enter an injured* CHRISTIAN, *and another uninjured.*]

FERNANDO.

Come forth, brother. Who has injured you?

CHRISTIAN.

An archí.[11]

FERNANDO.

The cause?

CHRISTIAN.

I gave none.

VIVANCO.

Is the wound deep?

CHRISTIAN.

I'm not sure; it was well struck, and will no doubt be mortal.

---

11. Arch janissaries, or *archíes*, were chief sergeants of the Algerian janissaries, charged with the economic administration of a batallion, as Canavaggio notes in his edition of the play.

SECOND CHRISTIAN.

I have a crueler one, and in a place where it can't be seen.

CAURALÍ.

Won't you tell me what this is about, Alí?

MOOR.

They've sighted a large armada on the main.

FERNANDO.

Is this true? Are you leaving, Effendi Cauralí?

[*Exit* CAURALÍ.]

MOOR.

The janissaries are killing captives if they find them, or abusing them in their harsh fury; and these shouts you hear come from fearful Jews.

GUILLERMO.

Everyone, be still! I think you're lying, Alí, for there was no news of an armada in Spain of late.

MOOR.

Well, this proof contradicts and disabuses you: for in faith they say that more than three hundred galleys are now in view, with pennants and flags, heading for Algiers.

GUILLERMO.

Perhaps this is an enchanted armada.

[*Enter the* WARDEN.]

WARDEN.

My heart strains in my chest, and I'm bursting with rage!

OSORIO.

What has happened, Effendi?

WARDEN.

I'm about to recount the cruelty, which rivals the greatest foolishness ever seen. The sun rose this morning, and its rays imprinted such shapes on the clouds, that, although they have lied before, I believed them. They formed an armada that approached quickly over the calm sea, to land in Algiers. The eyes that see it discern the bows, sterns, and oars of the feigned galleys so clearly that there are those who affirm and swear they saw the overseer give his order and the rower follow it all at once. Another claims to have seen your

dead prophet[12] in the crow's nest of a ship, depicted on a flag. The
smoke showed an empty, dark body so vividly, and the ears heard
fire and thunder so closely that for fear of the bullets a good number
hugged the ground: such was the fear they suffered. Because of these
shapes that the sun imprinted on the clouds with its rays, fear gave
shape to another thousand within us. We thought that that Don
Juan, whose valor was the first to check and rein in the Ottoman
bravery, was coming to put an honorable end to the ill-fated beginning that his valiant father launched under an unlucky star.[13] The
janissary archíes, who are always drunk, took to killing captives in
order to have fewer enemies, and if by chance the sun had delayed
in erasing its deceptions, none of you in here would be safe. The
wounded number twenty or more, and more than thirty are dead.
The sun has now undone the armada; go back to your games.

OSORIO.

We can scarcely follow such bloody amusements!

SECOND CHRISTIAN.

Then hear another, bloodier and more serious story. The Cadí, as
you know, has a child in his power of a young and tender age, named
Francisco. He has spent all of his effort, authority, and reason, a thousand promises and threats, a thousand diverse favors, to get this bap-
tized treasure to agree willingly to circumcision, of his own accord.
His effort has been in vain; his reason has not been able to imprint
human designs on this sacred heart. And so, we hear, affronted and
shamed, he has quenched his hellish rage with Francisco. He's tied to
a column, the very image of Christ, stained crimson from head to toe
in his own blood. I fear he must have expired, for even one beyond his
years and strength could not have resisted such cruel martyrdom.

FATHER.

Sweet half of my soul, oh son of my heart, hold on to life while this
wretch comes to see you! Be quick, lazy feet, on the street of bitterness; I shall see Pilate himself and a figure of Christ!

---

12. An image of Christ was on Don Juan's royal galley.

13. Charles V launched an ill-fated attack on Barbarossa's Algiers in 1541, in which perhaps
twelve thousand men and 150 ships were lost to a sudden storm. This ruinous defeat prefigured
the destruction of the so-called Invincible Armada (Garcés 23–24).

[*The* FATHER *exits.*]

SECOND CHRISTIAN.

Is that his father, gentlemen?

FERNANDO.

That wretch is his father, a gentleman and an excellent Christian—
we're from the same village. Let our celebrations end and our rejoicing cease, for captive plays always end in tragedy.

[*Exeunt omnes. Enter* ZARA, HALIMA, *and* COSTANZA.]

HALIMA.

Your father asked me, friend, to come right away to dress you.

ZARA.

May heaven curse his intent!

HALIMA.

You're marrying a king and you're disgruntled? It's well known that
Muley is a gentleman. You must have your sights set elsewhere.

ZARA.

There's no one to please or displease me, for I know nothing of love.

HALIMA.

Well, tonight you'll find out, with your husband's lessons, that love is
sweet and delicious.

ZARA.

You bring me bitter news!

HALIMA.

What a coy woman!

ZARA.

It's not coyness but anger: for I had determined not to get married
for now, until heaven set my fortune to a different tune.

HALIMA.

Quiet, for you will find yourself a queen.

ZARA.

I am not moved by such interest. I'd be more at ease with another,
lower state.

HALIMA.

I swear on my life, Zara, that you're in love. Now show me the pearls
you have, for I want to see how many strings I can make.

ZARA.

You can see them in there. Go in, and leave me a while, for I want to speak with Costanza.

HALIMA.

You'll enjoy the dance before long!

[*She exits.*]

COSTANZA.

Tell me, mistress, what this is all about. Does getting married bother you so, and to a king?

ZARA.

I cannot tell you so many things so quickly.

COSTANZA.

Where does your misplaced anger come from?

ZARA.

Quiet, don't let anyone hear. I'm a Christian, I'm a Christian!

COSTANZA.

Saint Mary help me!

ZARA.

That Lady must be the light and guiding star through the sea of my grief.

COSTANZA.

Who taught you our law?

ZARA.

There's no time for me to tell. I'm a Christian; see, friend, what use a Moorish king is to me. Tell me: Do you by chance know a ransomed captive who is a gentleman and a soldier?

COSTANZA.

What is his name?

ZARA.

I'm not safe here, and I fear some unlucky encounter.

COSTANZA.

Then let's go inside.

ZARA.

No doubt that will be better.

[*Exeunt. Enter the* KING, *the* CADÍ, *and the* WARDEN PASHA.]

CADÍ.

It was a strange case!

KING.

So strange that I don't know if the world's ever seen anything like it.

CADÍ.

Frightful squadrons shaped out of fantastic shadows have often been seen in the air, with all the artifice and skill with which the true ones attack on a blank field; the clouds have rained blood and mail, and pieces of scimitars and shields.

KING.

The Christians call those marvels, which sometimes appear; but I've never heard of the sun's rays touching the clouds and forming such a large armada, by chance, without any mystery.

WARDEN.

That's what I say; by faith, the trick has cost you more than thirty Christians.

KING.

It wouldn't matter unless they had run all of them through.

CADÍ.

The fright took the whip and the fury from my hands.

KING.

What were you doing?

CADÍ.

I was beating a Christian . . .

KING.

Why?

CADÍ.

He's young, and neither gifts, promises, nor threats can make a Moor of him.

KING.

Is he by chance the Spanish boy from the other day?

CADÍ.

The same.

KING.

Then don't tire yourself, for he's Spanish, and your tricks, rages, punishments, and promises will be powerless to bend his will. How poorly you know those stubborn, obstinate, fierce, ferocious, arrogant, headstrong, indomitable, and daring dogs! You'll see him dead before he becomes a Moor.

[*Enter a* MOOR *holding a captive.*]

What has this Christian done?

MOOR.

Just now, in a strange boat unlike any I'd seen before, almost a league out into the sea, just now I caught him.

KING.

In what way was the boat strange?

MOOR.

It was a raft made of sticks, supported by many large gourds, and he served as a mast, standing in the middle, with his arms as a yard, and in his hands a ripped shirt served as a sail.

KING.

When did you get on the boat?

CHRISTIAN.

At midnight.

KING.

Why couldn't you get farther from land in such a long time?

CHRISTIAN.

Sultan, it was good for nothing more than to prevent me from drowning, and I just trusted in heaven and in the wind that, good and furious by turns, might land the misshapen boat on any Christian shore, for no oar or sail could make it take a swift course.

KING.

In short, you're a Spaniard!

CHRISTIAN.

I don't deny it.

KING.

Well, I renege of what you don't deny.

[*Enter the* SEXTON *with a feigned baby in diapers, and behind him the* JEW *of the casserole.*]

Is this another boat?

JEW.

This Christian just stole my son from me.

CADÍ.

What does he want the child for?

SEXTON.

Isn't he a good one? So that they may ransom him, if they don't want me to raise him and teach him the Our Father. What do you say, Rachel or Zedekiah, Pharez, Sadoc, Zebulon or devil?

JEW.

This Spaniard, sire, is the ruin of our Jewry; nothing there is safe from his claws.

KING.

Tell me: Aren't you Spanish?

SEXTON.

Don't you know it already?

KING.

Who's your master?

SEXTON.

The *dabají* Morato.

KING.

Deal with him, on my life.

CADÍ.

On mine, you're exactly right in what you've said about the barbarous Spanish dogs.

[*Enter another* MOOR *with another* CHRISTIAN, *very ragged and with wounded legs.*]

KING.

Who's this one?

MOOR.

A Spaniard who has fled so many times by land, that this one makes twenty-one escapes.

KING.

If we gave audience for four days, all those who came would complain of Spaniards.

THE BAGNIOS OF ALGIERS

CADÍ.

A strange case!

KING.

Priest, return the child to this Jew, and do no harm to this Christian, for since he surrendered his body to such danger, his soul must be in great agony. And you, are you Spanish?

CHRISTIAN.

From Valencia.

KING.

Just try to flee again, and if they bring you back, I'll impale you.

SEXTON.

My lord, make this buggering Jew at least give me the pay I've lost by chasing him to rob him of this whoreson.

CADÍ.

He's right; take out forty ásperos and give them to the priest, who deserves them.

SEXTON.

Did you hear that, my Jewish friend?

JEW.

I heard just fine; but I don't have them here.

SEXTON.

Let's go home.

CADÍ.

With the Spaniards, all this and more goes on.

[*Exeunt omnes. Enter the* FATHER *alone.*]

FATHER.

Do I dare to go inside? Oh impertinent fear! Come now, for a stone that naturally approaches its center fears no obstacle.

[*A curtain is drawn;* FRANCISQUITO *is discovered tied to a pillar in whatever way is most conducive to pity.*]

FRANCISQUITO.

Won't they untie me, so that I can at least die normally?

FATHER.

No, for this way you imitate Christ even more. If you're headed to heaven, you must not sit on the ground; you go quicker like this.

FRANCISQUITO.

Oh father, come to me, for seeing you consoles me! Cold and frozen
Death, with its mortal agony, is making me leave you!

FATHER.

Breathe your soul into my mouth, so that it may pierce mine! Ah, he
dies!

FRANCISQUITO.

Farewell, for I die!

FATHER.

God, to whom you aspire, join us in the place for which I yearn!
How slowly he breathes, now he's breathed his last! Go in peace,
beautiful soul, and ask Him who made you fortunate, since you see
him now, to sustain us in His pure, holy, happy, and honorable faith!
Would that I knew the dunghill where they will bury you, o small
and holy relic, so that I could water my plant with my tears!

[*Exeunt. The wedding procession must enter in this fashion:* HALIMA,
with a veil over her face, in place of ZARA; *they carry her on a platform
on their shoulders, with music and lighted torches, guitars and song and
great rejoicing, singing the songs that I shall provide.*[14] VIVANCO *and*
LOPE *enter behind everyone, and among the Moorish musicians goes*
OSORIO, *the captive. As they pass by,* LOPE *asks* OSORIO:]

LOPE.

Who is this bride?

OSORIO.

Zara, Agimorato's daughter.

LOPE.

That's impossible!

OSORIO.

It's obvious!

VIVANCO.

Her face and the trappings of the wedding make it clear.

14. Here the stage direction recalls the difference between the author's intentions and the
actual fate of the unperformed plays.

OSORIO.

By God, gentlemen, it's her, and she's the most beautiful and richest Moor in Barbary!

LOPE.

By the veil she wore, we couldn't recognize her.

OSORIO.

Muley Maluco is to be her husband, the one who aspires to be king of Fez, a very famous Moor, well versed and attentive to his sect and evil law. He knows Turkish, Spanish, German, Italian, and French; he sleeps on a raised bed and eats at a table, sitting Christian-fashion. Most of all, he's a great soldier, generous, wise, composed, adorned with many graces.[15]

LOPE.

What do you think of this, my friend?

VIVANCO.

That we've bargained well, for with a pole for a staff, and Zara as a new Moses out of this depraved Egypt, we cross the dry sea to enjoy our dear homeland.

OSORIO.

The Jew spends his riches on holidays, the Moor, on weddings; the Christian, of his own will, follows a different rule, devoid of all pleasure,

[ZARA *appears at the window.*]

for he uses it up on lawsuits.

ZARA.

Psst! You, Christian slave!

OSORIO.

Farewell, gentlemen, for I want to see this to the very end!

LOPE.

I commend your taste.

ZARA.

Christian or Moorish enemy!

15. Muley Maluco ['Abd-el Malik], to whom the real-life Zara was engaged, became the sultan of Morocco in 1576 and ruled until 1578. The Spanish original uses the word *cristianesca*, which implies Moors who imitate Christian customs, as in this case.

VIVANCO.

Who calls us?

ZARA.

One who deserves to be heard.

LOPE.

By God, friend, her voice sounds like Zara!

VIVANCO.

I should say so.

ZARA.

Tell me what this rejoicing and celebration is about.

LOPE.

Muley Maluco is getting married to Zara, who lives here.

ZARA.

A foolish answer.

LOPE.

There she goes on a litter with music and merriment. Do you command something else?

ZARA.

I see now, Lela María, how you seek remedy for me.

LOPE.

Are you Zara?

ZARA.

I am Zara. You, who are you?

LOPE.

I've gone mad!

ZARA.

What are you saying?

LOPE.

That I am a slave who adores you, mistress. I am Don Lope.

ZARA.

I'll go let you in.

[*She disappears from the window and goes down to open the door.*]

VIVANCO.

It's not without its mystery that Zara is both here and there.

LOPE.

Her faith deserves this reward. Her being here all alone increases my wonder; where there are so many servants, she's found such seclusion; it's all a miracle and good fortune.

VIVANCO.

It's because of the rejoicing and merriment of the wedding. He who makes her appear in different places can do much more than this to remove the obstacles to the good that must follow.

[*Enter* ZARA.]

Do you see where she appears, Lope? Tell me if it's not right to take this treasure from Mohammed.

LOPE.

Oh Love most extreme, who tames the soul! Remedy in my sickness, support in my fall, freedom from my prison, happy life in my death, credit to my truth, repository of all peace from my battles, sun that lights up my senses, beacon that guides lost wretches home— see me here prostrate at your feet, all the more your slave and more vanquished than when I lay in chains; lost and won by you, at once imprisoned and free; give me your divine feet and your hands, worthy of Alexander, where I might set my lips!

ZARA.

It's not good for Christian lips to be sullied by Moorish women. You have seen by a thousand signs that I am all yours, not for you but for Christ. And so, to prove that I am His, I resist these caresses. Save them for another time, for now, when the soul trembles with a thousand fears, it cannot await or attend to the niceties of love. When do you leave for Spain, and when do you intend to return for one who remains, yet follows you? When will you accomplish such a glorious deed? When will your eyes look again on the Moorish spoils that long to be Christian? When will you end my fears and troubles with the sight of you?

LOPE.

I shall leave tomorrow, mistress; within eight days I believe I shall return, for I know that they will be centuries when longing counts them. Be in your father's garden, where you shall see how I keep my faith and word, though it cost me the life your sight gives me. And do not worry that I shall fail you in this, for heaven cannot wish to deny its help on earth to such an honest case. I am a Christian and a Spaniard, and a gentleman, and I give you my faith and my word again to do what I must.

ZARA.

I'm quite satisfied, but if you love me well, so that I feel more certain, swear to me by Marién.

LOPE.

I swear by the Immaculate Virgin, and by her Son as well, never to forget you and to do what you shall see for my pleasure and your benefit!

ZARA.

You've sworn a strong oath! Enough; swear no more to me.

VIVANCO.

What does your father say about your marriage to Muley Maluco?

ZARA.

Tonight I made a complaint with which I undid the wedding. He had ordered me today to adorn myself to be a bride tonight; he came and found me in tears, left without wanting to speak to me, and throughout the city it is said that I'm getting married tonight.

VIVANCO.

That's true.

LOPE.

This is a miracle! Don't worry her any more; keep quiet. Give me your hands, mistress, until such a time as you give them with your embraces.

ZARA.

No, give me your feet instead, for you're Christian and I'm a Moor. Go in peace, for while you go and come back, I shall pray to blessed heaven with the words of my faith and the tears of my lament, begging it to calm the sea, to smooth the wind, constant and favorable in your sails, to free you from harm, and to sharpen my mind in its faith. Farewell, for I cannot stay longer. Tomorrow I'll go to the garden, where I'll await you.

VIVANCO.

You'll see a happy ending to this beginning.

ZARA.

Are you leaving me and going away?

LOPE.

I can do nothing else.

ZARA.

Will that happy hour ever come in which I see you again?

[*Exit* ZARA.]

LOPE.

It will come, if Death is not harsh, as is its way. It would not be wise to leave until I see the end of this figured wedding.

VIVANCO.

The mystery it holds ensures my success.

[*Exeunt. A nuptial bed is discovered on which* HALIMA *lies, her face covered with a veil; they dance the morisca;*[16] *there are torches about;* DON LOPE *and* VIVANCO *watch, and, when the dance is over, two* MOORS *enter.*]

FIRST MOOR.

Let the celebration cease, and the lovely Zara return to her house, for Muley orders it thus, with admirable prudence.

SECOND MOOR.

Then the wedding won't go forth?

FIRST MOOR.

Yes, it will, but he wishes Zara to remain in her father's house, pure and untouched, while he procures his kingdom in Morocco; for thus she will be safer, and he hopes to enjoy her at leisure in his kingdom. Before the sun rises he will set out on this enterprise; the two thousand janissaries in his camp make him hurry, for you know he is on the march.

SECOND MOOR.

If that was his intention, why did he want Zara promenaded about? What will the people say? No doubt they'll think that he no longer wants to marry her.

---

16. The *morisca* was a dance common to Mediterranean Europe that imitated a conflict between Moors and Christians, much like the popular festival called *moros y cristianos*. What is fascinating in this case is that stage Moors are dancing the *morisca*.

FIRST MOOR.

Let them say what they will, this is his pleasure, and we can only
keep quiet and obey. What's more, Agimorato agrees.

SECOND MOOR.

Is she to return with ceremony?

FIRST MOOR.

By no means!

SECOND MOOR.

Let's bring her back, then.

VIVANCO.

O Almighty God!

[*Everyone exits and the curtain closes over the wedding bed;*
DON LOPE *and* VIVANCO *remain on stage.*]

Your mysteries are great! Now you can go with confidence, for you
see how easily this illusion and shadow has come undone.

LOPE.

They're premises of our success. I'm going to embark. Mind you go
to the place I've told you to, and signal again each night after six days
have passed, which is when I plan to return, I hope. And procure
with cunning and counsel, without ever betraying your intent, that
the father of that martyr take refuge in the garden with another
friend, for if the ship on which I sail stops in Majorca, I may well see
you again within six days.

VIVANCO.

Go with God, and I'll make sure that more than two gain their freedom. Don't forget the signals. Embrace me, and good courage. Be
diligent, and God guide you.

LOPE.

Don't confide this secret to anyone.

[*Exeunt. Enter* OSORIO *and the* SEXTON.]

OSORIO.

The story's the most comical I ever heard—that the Jews themselves
ransomed you out of their own money.

SEXTON.

It happened just as I tell you: amusingly, they've ransomed and freed me. They say that in this way they secure their children, their stuff and casseroles, and finally, all their wealth. I've given my word not to rob them of anything while I make my way to Spain, and by God, I don't know if I'll keep it.

[*Enter a* CHRISTIAN.]

CHRISTIAN.

The alms have arrived in Bejaia,[17] Christians.

OSORIO.

This is good news! Who has come?

CHRISTIAN.

The Order of Mercy.

OSORIO.

God grant it to us! And who is in charge?

CHRISTIAN.

I'm told it's a prudent man named Fray Jorge de Olivar.[18]

SEXTON.

May he be welcome!

OSORIO.

A certain Fray Rodrigo de Arce[19] has been here at other times, and he's of the same order, a noble soul of high worth.

SEXTON.

At least I'm spared reverences and prayers, thanks to Zedekiah and to Rabbi Nephtali, who gave the money. It was good to hope, but it's better to have. What's done is very well done; and the alms may arrive when they please. O bells of Spain! When will I hold your clappers in these hands? When will I make the *ding* and *dong* or the solemn ascent? When will I see my coffer filled with the rolls that the

17. According to Haedo's *Topographia*, Bejaia was thirty leagues east of Algiers (approximately 200 km). As Canavaggio's edition notes, it was controlled by Spaniards between 1509 and 1555. Alms would reach Algiers with the expeditions of the Mercedarian and Trinitarian orders, which were dedicated to the redemption of Christian captives. Ransom funds for these expeditions came from both private and public sources and were a favorite cause for Spanish charities (Friedman 110).

18. A Mercedarian friar working for the Aragonese crown, he rescued Cervantes's brother Rodrigo in 1577 (Cervantes 1998, 14:136).

19. Another Mercedarian friar from Toledo who commanded the order's province in Castile.

rich widows give in remembrance of the poor departed ones? When, oh when?

CHRISTIAN.

Where are you going now?

OSORIO.

Agi Morato invited the Cadí to go to his garden for three or four days; for he plans to spend all summer there with his daughter Zara and the beautiful Halima, Caouralí's consort.

CHRISTIAN.

Perhaps one day I'll go and amuse myself with you there a while.

OSORIO.

You'll be well received.

CHRISTIAN.

Farewell, friends!

SEXTON.

Since I'm free, I'll also go to see you, Osorio.

OSORIO.

Then bring the guitar, and if possible, come soon.

SEXTON.

I shall.

> [*Exeunt.* Enter HALIMA, ZARA, COSTANZA, *and as she comes*
> *in* ZARA *drops a rosary, which* HALIMA *picks up.*]

HALIMA.

What's this, Zara my friend? A cross on your beads?[20]

COSTANZA.

Those are mine.

HALIMA.

If this isn't devotion, I don't know what to think or say.

ZARA.

What is a cross?

HALIMA.

This stick that intersects this other one.

ZARA.

Well then: What is that sign?

---

20. See Act II, note 16, for further discussion of Christian and Muslim prayer beads.

HALIMA.

Your dissimulation isn't bad! It's a sign that the Christians worship as we do Allah.

COSTANZA.

Mistress, give it to me, for it's mine.

HALIMA.

Your effort is in vain, for Zara dropped it, and I saw it with my own eyes.

ZARA.

Don't let this upset you. Costanza gave it to me when I was in your house the other day, and I don't know what a cross is.

COSTANZA.

That's how it was, and it was careless of me not to take that sign away from her. Yet is it unseemly in your Moorish prayer?

ZARA.

G'Allah, she is not wrong.

HALIMA.

Be that as it may, take it off, sister; for if a Moor sees it, he'll say that you secretly keep the Christian faith.

[*Enter* VIVANCO *and* DON FERNANDO.]

VIVANCO.

I've confided this secret in you as you're a gentleman.

FERNANDO.

I hope to be grateful by being discreet. These are Halima and Zara, for I know them well.

VIVANCO.

Our plan's going well.

HALIMA.

Look, friend, look: here comes my Christian, and in him comes the enemy whom I adore and curse.

ZARA.

What do you mean?

HALIMA.

I can no longer pretend.

COSTANZA.

Woe is me! And if she wants to declare herself to him?

HALIMA.

I want to speak to him.

COSTANZA.

It's useless to resist Love.

ZARA.

Do you love him?

HALIMA.

May he pardon my shame: I adore him, and he knows it, and I don't know how to conquer his hardness.

ZARA.

And he does not soften with you?

HALIMA.

Constanza says he does; but I've always seen the harshness of an enemy in him. Come here; tell me, Christian, do you know that you're my captive?

FERNANDO.

Yes, mistress, and I know that I live for you.

HALIMA.

How now, you monster? Haven't my eyes and Costanza's tongue ever told you that the end of my hopes is in your power? Have you been waiting for me to go through this painful experience in front of so many, showing you my wound? What an unfortunate faith this is, for what they call love is now a blaze, now a fury, and has no regard for anything. Beware, for if you scorn what I say, man, you might well make an enemy of such a friendly woman.

FERNANDO.

I only ask three days' term, my lady, to give the sweet ending that you shall see to your persistence. Go with God to Zara's garden and wait for me there: as I've said, your fierce grief will come to a sweet end.

HALIMA.

I am content!

ZARA.

And I pledge by my hand that he shall do as he says.

COSTANZA.

This is very well arranged!

HALIMA.

If you must come, come early.

ZARA.

What is this wind that blows, Christian?

VIVANCO.

The north wind, it seems, and with it the one who guides and aids us brings good fortune.

ZARA.

Has your friend already left for Spain?

VIVANCO.

It must be six days ago now.

ZARA.

Would you remain here alone without him?

VIVANCO.

I was alone, but I hope to see him soon.

ZARA.

How soon?

VIVANCO.

I would leave tomorrow if there were a ship.

HALIMA.

Christian, look up. What is this? You're very melancholic. What's wrong? What do you feel? Tell me.

COSTANZA.

Let us leave here, my lady, though I must die where you're going, for my heart is pounding through my chest.

ZARA.

It must be from waking up so early.

COSTANZA.

And from having had a vision— if it's true, if it's reasonable—that will end my life today.

FERNANDO.

These are all vain illusions; there's nothing to fear, Costanza.

COSTANZA.

I'll find out soon.

ZARA.

Christian women are so fearful!

COSTANZA.

Not so, though there are some who are frightened by the heavens. I was about to say jealousy, and I wouldn't have been far off.[21]

HALIMA.

Allah be with you, my Fernando, and be sure to come right away, I command and beg you.

COSTANZA.

It's enough to say, "I command you."

[*The three ladies exit.*]

VIVANCO.

Let's go; perhaps fortune will have been so favorable that Don Lope will have arrived already. We shouldn't miss our opportunity.

[*Exit* VIVANCO *and* DON FERNANDO. *Enter the* FATHER *with a bloodied white handkerchief, in which he carries the bones of* FRANCISQUITO.]

FATHER.

I'll have Osorio guard them. I fear that this darkness will either confuse me or make me late. Oh how typical it is of one my age to be timid and cowardly! Yet my feet will walk these holy relics to Agimorato's garden. Great care must be taken where there are so many snares.

[*Exits. Enter* DON FERNANDO *and* VIVANCO.]

VIVANCO.

He's at sea, no doubt: for this broken plate shows he came ashore. Let him come to our signal: strike the flint, friend, and make from it the light that brings, guides, and lights the remedy for our trouble.

FERNANDO.

Don't you see how other sparks respond to ours?

VIVANCO.

Such happy signs are not sparks but stars. Hush, and listen to the soft sound of the holy oars.

FERNANDO.

Let's get closer to the shore. There's no doubt: it's them.

[*Enter* DON LOPE *and the* CAPTAIN *of the boat.*]

21. Here the original puns on *celo* (jealousy) and *cielo* (heaven).

LOPE.

Is it Vivanco?

VIVANCO.

The same.

LOPE.

Is Zara in the garden?

VIVANCO.

Yes, friend.

LOPE.

Today heaven grants a happy ending to my troubles!

VIVANCO.

Embrace me!

LOPE.

There's no time for courtesies now. Go get her.

VIVANCO.

Right. You can't wait long.

FERNANDO.

Do you want me to go with you, friend?

VIVANCO.

There's no need: I'll bring them with me in a moment; they're all ready and waking, waiting for this.

LOPE.

Then rush, friend.

CAPTAIN.

Are they far off?

VIVANCO.

They're close by.

[Exits.]

CAPTAIN.

Oh let them not take too long, for the wind's favorable!

LOPE.

Be quiet, no one speak, for I hear a noise.

CAPTAIN.

Let's return to the boat until we see what it is, sir.

LOPE.

Shh, don't make a sound, for we're safe here.

[*Enter* VIVANCO, HALIMA,[22] ZARA, COSTANZA, *the* FATHER,
with a white handkerchief, to show that he carries the bones of
FRANCISQUITO; OSORIO, *the* SEXTON *and other*
CHRISTIANS *that could come out.*]

VIVANCO.

They were alert and saw the signals at sea, and, unable to wait for me, ran to the coast. They saved me the walk.

OSORIO.

This is miraculous fortune!

LOPE.

Where is my beautiful star?

ZARA.[23]

Where is my divine compass?

CAPTAIN.

This is no time for courtesies; embark, for the wind's picking up. O light and holy cargo, make the winds favorable!

SEXTON.

I was already ransomed, but I'll go for all that.

CAPTAIN.

Are there any more Christians?

FERNANDO.

I don't know.

VIVANCO.

I've gathered whom I could.

COSTANZA.

Let's go before Halima wakes up!

FERNANDO.

Do you want me to go back for her?

CAPTAIN.

Everyone get on the boat.

22. We have retained the stage direction of the Spanish original here: though Halima does not speak in this scene, she may be asleep with the other characters. The "other Christians" of the last phrase refers to the staging of the play, perhaps to minor characters such as the captive who repeatedly fails to escape.

23. This line has a history of misattribution. Modern editors inexplicably give the line to Halima, but the 1615 printed text gives it to Zara.

COSTANZA.

Does it pain you to leave your mistress?

FERNANDO.

I wish my master were here.

LOPE.

Let's go, Zara.

ZARA.

Zara no more, I am María now.

LOPE.

This business[24] was not taken from the imagination, for truth forged it far from fiction. This love story, of happy memory, survives in Algiers—thus should truth and history delight the understanding. And even today one may find the window and the garden there. And here this business comes to an end, though that of Algiers has none.

⊞   FINIS.   ⊞

---

24. Cervantes again puns on *trato* ("business, commerce") and the title of his earlier Algerian play, *El trato de Argel* (The Traffic of Algiers).

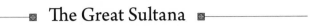

The Great Sultana

DRAMATIS PERSONAE

SALEC, *a renegade Turk*
ROBERTO, *a renegade*
An ARAB
The OTTOMAN SULTAN [*also the* TURK *or* GRAND SIGNOR]
A PAGE, *dressed in Turkish style, and three other* GARZONS
MAMÍ *and* RUSTÁN, *eunuchs*
DOÑA CATALANIA DE OVIEDO, *the Great Sultana*
Her FATHER
MADRIGAL, *a captive*
ANDREA, *a spy*
TWO JEWS
An AMBASSADOR *from Persia*
TWO MOORS
The GREAT CADÍ
Four old PASHAS
CLARA, *called* ZAIDA
ZELINDA, *who is* LAMBERTO
An old CAPTIVE
TWO MUSICIANS

Act I

[*Enter* SALEC, *a Turk, and* ROBERTO, *dressed as a Greek, and an* ARAB[1] *behind them, dressed in a mantle of rough cloth; he carries many bits of oakum on a lance and, on the end of a quince branch, a piece of paper like a note, and a small candle lit in his hand; this* ARAB *goes to the side of the stage, without speaking a word, and then* ROBERTO *says:*]

ROBERTO.

The splendor and majesty of this tyrant clearly extend beyond human power. But what apparition is this, his lance half covered with oakum? He seems an Arab by his dress.

SALEC.

The poor here have this custom when one comes to seek justice (which only interest can attain): he prepares a stick with oakum, and when the Turk passes by he sets it on fire. The Turk stops at its brightness; he loudly demands justice; the guards make way for him, and the poor man, like a dart, approaches in a fluster. On the tip of a stick he presents his petition to the Grand Signor, who pauses for that purpose. Then it is given to a handsome garzon,[2] who keeps track of these petitions and later recounts them; but these wretches' business never comes to a good end: interest holds sway, and they are denied.

ROBERTO.

I've seen such marvelous things here that the liveliest mind wonders at them.

SALEC.

You'll see even more striking things. The Grand Signor's already on foot; you can behold him at your pleasure, for a Christian can look

1. Cervantes here differentiates Arabs (*alárabes*) from North Africans (*moros*), though his characters sometimes conflate the two.
2. *Garzón*, the word used for the Sultan's pageboys, often means "catamite" in early modern Spain, especially when referring to the Ottomans or North Africa, as in *The Bagnios of Algiers*.

him in the face at his leisure. It's forbidden for any Moor or Turk to raise an eye to him, and in this he exceeds all majesty.

[*At this moment the* TURK[3] *enters with a large entourage; in front of him goes a* PAGE *dressed in the Turkish fashion, with an arrow in his upraised hand, and behind the* TURK *two other* GARZONS *follow with two green velvet sacks, in which they place the papers the* TURK *gives them.*]

ROBERTO.

He's certainly a good-looking young man, justly famed for his poise and elegance.

SALEC.

Today the Turk prays Salah[4] in St. Sophia, that temple you see there, greater than any other in Turkey.

ROBERTO.

The Moor sets his torch on fire and shouts; the Turk calmly stops, a sign of mercy and nobility. The Moor comes up to him; he's given him a petition; the Grand Signor takes it and gives it to a handsome garzon who's nearly beside him.

[*While* ROBERTO *is saying this and the* TURK *passes by,* SALEC *keeps his body bowed down and his head inclined, without looking at his face.*]

SALEC.

This audience is not denied to the poor. Can I raise my head?

ROBERTO.

Rise and look, for the Grand Signor is arriving at the mosque, whose greatness fills me with wonder even from here.

[*Exit the* GRAND SIGNOR. SALEC *and* ROBERTO *remain onstage.*]

SALEC.

What do you think, Roberto, of the splendor and majesty displayed here before you?

ROBERTO.

I can't believe the truth and doubt what's certain.

---

3. The "Great Turk" of the play, Sultan Murad III (1546–1595), also called Amurath or Amurates, ruled from 1574 to 1595. He was the son of Selim II, who was vanquished at Lepanto by the Sacred Alliance in 1571, and Nur Banu, the illegitimate daughter of the Venetian Nicolò Venier. The historical Murad fell in love with the Corfiote Christian captive Safidje. See Mas.

4. *Salah*, or prayer, is performed five times daily and is one of the five pillars of Islam.

SALEC.

There are six thousand soldiers on foot and on horseback.

ROBERTO.

So it appears.

SALEC.

There's no question; they number six thousand.

ROBERTO.

All together, they cause wonder, pleasure, and dread.

SALEC.

When he goes to Salah he brings this entourage with him; and it's the day of *xumá*,[5] as the Moors call Friday.

ROBERTO.

He is well accompanied! Now, since we have some time, I want to finish what I started telling you yesterday.

SALEC.

Begin again, friend.

ROBERTO.

I've come to seek that young man of whom I spoke: for I love him more than the soul that sustains me, more than my very eyes. Ever since he was very young, I was his tutor and teacher, and showed him the narrow road to the temple of fame; I set his steps on the narrow path of virtue; I kept his youthful desires in check. But my well-considered advice, my Christian badgering, a thousand examples of good and evil, were not enough to prevent Love, that *monfí*[6] of youth, from assaulting him in his tender age.

He fell in love with Clara, the daughter of Lamberto, that German nobleman whom you met in Prague. Her parents and her beauty gave her the name of Clara;[7] but now her misfortunes have cast a shadow over her. He asked for her hand in marriage but did not succeed in his attempt, not because the marriage was unequal or

5. *Xumá*: Arabic, "Jumu'ah," communal Friday *Salah* services held shortly after noon in a mosque.

6. *Monfí*: a Spanish word from the Arabic meaning "highwayman" or "bandit," especially a Moorish one.

7. The name Clara implies brightness, purity, and clarity.

misguided, but because misfortunes come from afar, and there is no human diligence that can prevent them.

To conclude: he carried her off, for when wills are set on pleasure they lose all respect and fear. Alone and on foot on a cold winter's night the poor lovers fled they knew not where, and by the time I had noticed the absence of Lamberto (for that is the name of the wretch I come to seek), I saw him before me, faint of breath, face covered in cold sweat, and much distressed. He threw himself at my feet, his color like a dead man's, and with a voice racked by sobs said: "I'm dying, my father and lord, for these names I owe you. The Turks of Rocaferro[8] have taken Clara captive. I, a coward, a wretch, and a traitor—I can't deny it—have left her in their hands, since I was fleet of foot. This very night I was taking her I know not where, but I do know that, if Fortune had willed it, we'd both be in heaven." At this sad news, I was left in confused silence, without daring to ask him: "My son, how could this happen?" The martial din of the alarm sounded by the town bells brought me out of my puzzlement. I mounted straightaway, Lamberto did the same, and a whole troop of armored horses set out. The dark made us lose the trace of those who took Clara, and others whose absence was noticed at daybreak. Fearing an ambush, we didn't stray far from the town, to which we returned exhausted and without Lamberto.

SALEC.

How? Did he stay back on purpose?

ROBERTO.

On purpose, I suspect, for he hasn't shown up since, dead or alive. Clara's father offered a huge sum for her, but he could not get her back at any price. It was said that the Turk who owned her had presented her to the Grand Signor for her great beauty. To find out if this is true, and for word of Lamberto, I've come here, as you see, dressed as a Greek. I speak the language well enough to pass as one.

SALEC.

Even if you'd never learned it, you needn't worry: here all is confusion, and we make ourselves understood in a mixed language that

8. We have been unable to find information on this location.

we both know and don't know.[9] But you won't escape from me; I recognized you the moment I saw you.

ROBERTO.

An excellent memory!

SALEC.

It was always good.

ROBERTO.

How, then, have you forgotten who you are?

SALEC.

Let's not discuss that now: tomorrow we'll talk of my affairs; for, truth be told, I don't believe in anything.

ROBERTO.

You seem a fine atheist.

SALEC.

I know not how I seem; all I know is that I will clearly show you, through my works, that I'm your friend just as before. To learn of Clara, a eunuch from the Turk's household will serve—he's my friend. Meanwhile, you can look for Lamberto: perhaps his body is now a prisoner, as his soul once was.

[*Exeunt. Enter* MAMÍ *and* RUSTÁN, *eunuchs*].

MAMÍ.

Keep your mouth shut, Rustán, and don't use me to back up your word, empty of all truth. You lie in everything you say, and there's no doubt you're a Christian. Keeping the captive Spaniard locked away like this for so long and concealing her is proof enough of your bad intentions. You've kept the Grand Signor from enjoying the greatest beauty in the world. It is wrong to give him ripe fruit when unripened is better. For six years you've hidden her and shielded her with precautions that can last no longer, and now you go to great lengths to reveal her? But just wait, you dog, hold on, and you'll see how one keeps faith with the Grand Signor!

---

9. In several texts, such as *Don Quixote* and *El amante liberal* (The Generous Lover), Cervantes discusses the lingua franca of captivity—a mix of tongues from the Mediterranean, including Portuguese, Spanish, Italian, and others. See Haedo, chapter 29, for a description.

RUSTÁN.

Mamí, my friend, wait, wait!

MAMÍ.

Punishment comes, even if it takes time. One who knows of treachery and yet does not reveal it at once seems partly to condone it. I've discovered yours today, and so I shall go to the Grand Signor to tell him of your wrongdoing.

[*He exits.*]

RUSTÁN.

There's no denying it: I am as good as impaled.

[*Enter* DOÑA[10] CATALINA DE OVIEDO, *the Great Sultana, dressed in the Turkish fashion.*]

SULTANA.

What news, Rustán?

RUSTÁN.

My lady, the hour of our untimely death has come: my soul is warning me, for it weeps despite my resolve. For though I seem like a woman, I never shed tears for a great good or ill, as is often the case. My lady, Mamí, with cleverness and wicked intent, has found out how long I have kept you hidden, and has judged my loyalty for treachery and for sin. He's headed directly to the Grand Signor to tell the tale of evil I held to be good, his wicked heart ever full of malice and rage.

SULTANA.

What shall we do?

RUSTÁN.

Await death with what integrity we can muster, although I know the Sultan will respect your beauty. He won't kill you; Rustán will be the one to die, as the author of this case.

SULTANA.

Is the Grand Signor cruel?

---

10. As with Doña Costanza in *The Bagnios of Algiers*, Catalina's nobility is important in the play. Cervantes is careful to preserve class distinctions in both Spanish and Ottoman societies.

RUSTÁN.

They call him gentle, but he's really a tyrant.

SULTANA.

With all this, I trust in God, whose powerful hand will free us both from this justifiable fear. And if the heavens be closed to me because of my sins, and do not hear my request, I shall ready my heart for a more terrible outcome. This inhumane one will not triumph over my soul, only over my body, which is weak, fragile, and vain.

RUSTÁN.

I feared my Christian behavior would lead to this. But I'm not sorry; rather, I'm armed with patience and forbearance against any torture.

SULTANA.

We're of the same mind. I'm prepared to accept as a gift any punishment that befalls me.

RUSTÁN.

Such beauty is never condemned to death. Your loveliness will bring you not punishment but good fortune; I, on the other hand, will find my grave in the fire, I fear.

SULTANA.

Though the world offer me all the treasures of the earth and sea, though the peerless Enemy make war on me with legions of his infernal squadron, they will not change my good intentions, my Lord, for I trust in you. At a tender age, I lost, dear God, my liberty, which I hardly knew. The beauty you gave me, Lord, brought me here. If it is to be the instrument of my undoing, I consent—a Christian and sane hope—to losing my beauty instantly, by a miracle. This rosy hue my flattering mirror shows—wither it with your right hand; make me ugly, Lord; for the beauty of the body should not surpass the soul's.

RUSTÁN.

You're right. But we should not tarry here, without making a plan or finding a way to excuse or remedy our fault.

SULTANA.

There is a great distance between remedy and excuse. Let's prepare ourselves, friend, to die like Christians.

RUSTÁN.

That's the most important remedy that you can ask of heaven.

[*Exeunt. Enter* MAMÍ, *the eunuch, and
the* GRAND SIGNOR.]

MAMÍ.

Morato Arráez,[11] Grand Signor, presented her to you, and she takes the first and the best prize for beauty. Rustán's efforts have kept this great treasure hidden from your eyes for six years, going on seven, by my count.

TURK.

And is she as beautiful as you've said?

MAMÍ.

She is as lovely as the fresh blooming rose untouched by the sun in a closed garden; or as the serene dawn, full of dewdrops and pearls, when it rises from the bright east; or as the sun in the west, with the reflections it forms. Nature stole the best part of everything to make this piece, and so made her lovely beyond human beauty. She took two stars from the sky to place as beautiful lights for her most beautiful eyes, which makes love more powerful, since it abides in them. The whole and its parts go together so well that perfection attends them both. And her color is no less, which makes her whole shape immensely pleasing.

TURK.

This fool must be describing some goddess.

MAMÍ.

Her beauty, which is so great that it defies imagination, is surpassed by her discretion.

SULTAN.

You'll have me worship her as something holy and divine.

MAMÍ.

The sun has never seen one like her, nor did heaven forge another

---

11. A famed renegade corsair of Albanian origin: a common reference of the period, he also figures in *The Bagnios of Algiers* (see Act I, note 8).

in its crucible. Above all, it conferred upon her the Spanish grace. I mean, my lord, that this captive's beauty is divine, rare in the world.

TURK.

My desire to see her grows. Her name?

MAMÍ.

Catalina, her last name de Oviedo.

TURK.

Why hasn't she changed her name, now that she is a Turk?

MAMÍ.

I don't know; since she hasn't changed her faith, she desires no other name.

TURK.

So she is a Christian?

MAMÍ.

I find that she is.

TURK.

A Christian, in my seraglio?

MAMÍ.

There must be more than a few; but who could prove it? If I knew of anything else like this, I'd tell you, without concealing for a minute any word or deed or thought against you.

TURK.

This is your carelessness and evil.

MAMÍ.

I tell you I worship and serve you with the loyalty and due decorum I owe Your Majesty.

TURK.

I shall go to the seraglio this afternoon, to see if the unparalleled beauty of your exalted Spaniard chills or burns.

MAMÍ.

May Mohammed keep you, my lord.

> [*Exeunt. Enter* MADRIGAL, *a captive, and* ANDREA,
> *dressed as a Greek.*]

MADRIGAL.

By Roch,[12] you dogs in caps, you won't enjoy that *boronía* stew with beef broth![13]

ANDREA.

Who are you yelling at, Christian?

MADRIGAL.

Not at nobody. Can't you hear the racket and war cries[14] from this house?

[A JEW *says from within:]*

JEW.

Oh dog! May G-d curse and confound you! May you never attain your beloved liberty!

ANDEA.

Tell me: why do those wretches curse you?

MADRIGAL.

I got into their house without being seen and threw a big hunk of bacon into a large pot they had of a stew called *boronía*.

ANDREA.

But who gave it to you?

MADRIGAL.

Some janissaries killed a wild boar in the forest the other day, which they sold to Mamud Arráez's Christians, from whom I bought part of the jowl that's now sunk in the pot to sink these wretches whom I resent. May the devil eat, devour, and sip them up!

[A JEW *appears at the window.]*

JEW.

May you die of hunger, you insolent barbarian! May G-d deny you your daily bread; may you wander from door to door begging; may they send you away from this place like a leper, you pest, you bogey-

---

12. Invoking St. Roch—commonly against plague—was a frequent euphemistic curse in early modern Spanish.

13. Madrigal invents the insulting adjective *barretina*—"hatted"—based on the cap early modern Jews wore. *Boronía* stew, like the *mojí* casserole in *The Bagnios of Algiers*, was prepared on Friday to be consumed on the Sabbath the next day (Martínez López 128). *Boronía* contained eggplant, tomatoes, squash, and pepper (Cervantes 1998, 15:37).

14. Covarrubias defines *algaraza* ("war cries" in our translation) as the shouting that Moors utter when ambushing Christians or other enemies (85).

man, scourge and fear of our synagogue, our children's enemy, our worst in the whole world!

MADRIGAL.

Look out, Jew!

JEW.

Oh no, he got me right between the eyes! O wretch!

ANDREA.

You didn't do that.

MADRIGAL.

The thought didn't even cross my mind!

ANDREA.

So what's the bastard complaining about?

> [*From within, another* JEW *says:*]

SECOND JEW.

Get away from the window, Zabulón, for that Spanish dog's a devil, and will break your head open just by spitting on you and hitting his mark. Alas, what a meal we have! Alas, what a stew is lost here!

MADRIGAL.

Are you wailing at Ramah again,[15] miserable rabble? Are you back once more, you dog?

SECOND JEW.

What! Haven't you gone yet? Perhaps you want to poison the air we breathe?

MADRIGAL.

Catch this one!

> [*They speak within.*]

Zabulón, is it no use telling you to stay out of the window? Let him go already; come inside, son.

ANDREA.

O ruined people! O vile and filthy race, what misery your fruitless waiting has brought you, your madness and incomparable obstinacy, which you call persistence and unwavering faith, against all truth and reason! Now it seems they quiet down; now the wretches suffer their hunger and trick in silence. Spaniard, do you know me?

---

15. Madrigal refers to Rachel's lamentations for her absent children in Jeremiah 31:15.

MADRIGAL.

I'd swear I've never seen you in my life.

ANDREA.

I'm Andrea, the spy.

MADRIGAL.

You're Andrea?

ANDREA.

Yes, absolutely.

MADRIGAL.

The one that saved Castillo and Palomares, my comrades?

ANDREA.

And the one that took Meléndez, Arguijo, and Santisteban, all at once, and left them at their ease in Naples, enjoying their liberty.

MADRIGAL.

How did you know me?

ANDREA.

Your memory's gone to rot, as far as I can tell, or been reduced to no good purposes. Don't you remember that I saw you and spoke to you the night I picked up those five, and you wanted to stay solely for your pleasure, with the excuse that your soul had surrendered to love, and that an Arab woman had imprisoned and chained it in a new captivity and new laws?

MADRIGAL.

True; and I still have the yoke around my neck, I'm still captive, the great power of love still rules over me.

ANDREA.

So it would be pointless to try to get you to come with me now?

MADRIGAL.

Completely pointless.

ANDREA.

You hapless man!

MADRIGAL.

Perhaps happy.

ANDREA.

How can that be?

MADRIGAL.

The laws of pleasure are very powerful.

ANDREA.

A strong resolve can break them.

MADRIGAL.

True; but it's not the time to fight them.

ANDREA.

Aren't you Spanish?

MADRIGAL.

Why? Because of this? Well, by the eleven thousand coats of mail,
and by the high, sweet, potent desire under the collar of four rich
boarders,[16] I swear that I will break through mountains of diamonds
and unspeakable obstacles, and I shall hoist my liberty on the very
shoulders of my pleasure, and enter triumphant into the beautiful
Naples with two or three galleys that will have rebelled because of
my cleverness and valor, and God willing, after giving two ships to
the Annunziata,[17] I'll live rich and prosperous with the other one,
instead of wandering through the bagnios weighted down with misery and dread.

ANDREA.

You're a Spaniard, there's no question!

MADRIGAL.

Indeed, I am, I am, I have been and shall be while I live, and eighty
centuries after I die.

ANDREA.

Does anyone want to escape to freedom?

MADRIGAL.

Four valiant soldiers await you, and they're well-born, with feathers
in their caps.

---

16. Madrigal's exaggerated rhetoric in this speech plays on the phrase *once mil*, meaning
both the number 11,000 and, in thieves' argot, a coat of mail. It may also allude to the legend of
the eleven thousand virgin martyrs supposedly buried with St. Ursula in Cologne.

17. Annunziata: the Chiesa della Santissima Annunziata in Naples. Freed captives would
often place chains, oars, and other remnants of their captivity in churches to give thanks.

ANDREA.

Are they the ones Arguijo mentioned?

MADRIGAL.

The same.

ANDREA.

I have them safe and hidden.

MADRIGAL.

What mob is this? What's that noise?

ANDREA.

It's the Persian ambassador, who has come to make peace with the Sultan. Move over here while he passes.

[*Enter an* AMBASSADOR, *dressed like those that travel around here,*[18] *accompanied by janissaries; he is dressed as a Turk.*]

MADRIGAL.

How brave and gallant he looks!

ANDREA.

Most of the Persians are brave, and well built, and great horsemen.

MADRIGAL.

And, as they say, the horses are the sinews of their strength. May it please God no peace be made! Are you coming, Andrea?

ANDREA.

Take me wherever you like.

MADRIGAL.

I'm going to Uchalí's bagnio.

ANDREA.

Take me to Morato's, for I have to meet another spy there.

[*Exeunt. Enter the* TURK, RUSTÁN, *and* MAMÍ.]

TURK.

You give me but a weak excuse for the treachery you've committed against me, the greatest ever seen.

---

18. Ambassadors of the shah Abbas I of Persia (1571–1629) included Robert Sherley, brother to Anthony Sherley, an Englishman who reformed the shah's army. Neither Spain nor England formed an alliance with the Persians, who wanted to join forces to defeat the Ottomans. For fuller discussion, see Chew, chapter 6. In 1599, the shah's ambassadors came to Spain and visited Valladolid, Madrid, Segovia, Toledo, and elsewhere.

RUSTÁN.

When you understand the facts, my lord, you will not blame me.
When she came into my power she would not have pleased you, and
it was better to keep her until she grew worthier. For many years,
Great Signor, her deep melancholy left her pale.

TURK.

Who cured her?

RUSTÁN.

Zedequías, the Jew, your doctor.

TURK.

You present dead witnesses in your favor; I'm sure you're trying to
get out of this.

RUSTÁN.

I'm telling the whole truth.

TURK.

So therefore you will not lie.

RUSTÁN.

It's barely been three days since the serene heaven of her face
showed itself full of beauty, barely three days since an anxious care
left her bosom. Indeed: it hasn't been three days since the Spaniard,
peerless in her beauty, broke free of her melancholy.

TURK.

You're lying or rambling.

RUSTÁN.

I neither lie nor ramble. You can see for yourself whenever you like,
my lord. Have her come to you: you'll see her grace and pluck; you'll
see heaven in her elegance, walking the earth on human feet.

TURK.

One fear follows another, one worry another worry. I fear much,
I hope much, for praise works wonders on a flatterer's tongue; but
flattery does not obtain here. Rustán, I want to see this captive now;
go and get her, and by the blind god[19] that amazes me, if she's not as
you've described, I'll give you to the fire!

19. The blind god: Cupid, or Eros.

[RUSTÁN *exits.*]

MAMÍ.

If Rustán's fortune lies in nothing more than the captive being beautiful, and of a rare beauty, he is a happy man; he's free from misfortune. You may start granting him favors, my lord, for soon you shall see the very heavens.

TURK.

Fool, you exceed all hyperbole. Leave something for the eyes to find in such divine spoils.

MAMÍ.

What eyes could gaze upon the red rays of Apollo and not be dazzled?

TURK.

So much praise annoys me.

MAMÍ.

Then I defer to your experience of her, whom my tongue aggrieves.

[*Enter* RUSTÁN *and the* SULTANA.]

RUSTÁN.

Speak to him gently and softly, my lady, so that he does not do away with all of us.

SULTANA.

I'll give the key to my tongue to heaven above; I'll throw myself at his feet; I'll say that I am his slave, whose great fortune it is to kiss his feet.

RUSTÁN.

A wise artifice.

SULTANA.

My knees bent and my eyes on yours, my lord, I give you the spoils my humble self comprises; and if it's arrogant to look upon you, I lower my eyes and follow the path that pleases you most.

TURK.

Ignorant, foolish people, fit, no doubt, to be tied! One could not find any more simpleminded; you who take away the fame such a high subject commands, liars, indeed! Treachery dishonors you! Any punishment would suit you well!

MAMÍ.

What bad luck for us if she seems ugly to him!

TURK.

How humanly you spoke of a divine loveliness, and how vulgarly you depicted this singular beauty! Wouldn't it have been better to put her at Allah's side, treading the elements and one or another bright star, issuing laws from thence, which we shall keep on earth with the same reverence and zeal as those Mohammed gave?

MAMÍ.

Didn't I tell you she was a blooming rose in the garden? What more could the most ingenious tongue say? Didn't I describe her as more prudent than has ever been seen before? Could a lying poet tell you more?

RUSTÁN.

I made her a heaven on human feet, my lord.

TURK.

You would have been right if you had made her its Maker.

RUSTÁN.

Not that: for those great qualities apply only to God.

TURK.

In her praise you were both too succinct and fell short, for which, without appeal, I will impale you before the day's over. You deserve a greater punishment, traitor Rustán, for keeping such a great treasure hidden from me for three days. For three days you have stopped the course of my fortune; for three days I've been tormented and uncertain; for three days you have cheated me of the greatest good on earth and under the sun. By all means, you shall die today, this very day: for your fortune will end where mine begins.

SULTANA.

If this captive has found some grace before you, let Rustán and Mamí live.

TURK.

Let Rustán die and Mamí live. Yet cursed be the tongue that spoke such a thing; you demand, I do not grant. I shall make up this lack by swearing an oath to you, by all my strength, not to waver one bit from your command. Not only shall Rustán live; if you so desire, you shall free the captives in the dungeons; for my will is as subject to yours as darkness is to the light of day.

SULTANA.

I'm not worthy of such a boon, my lord.

TURK.

Love makes you one with majesty. I see all of my kingdoms, which are nearly infinite, delivered to your jurisdiction; now my great dominions, which have made me a great lord, are yours more than mine by justice and by right. Do not wonder, "I am this; I was that," for, since you control me, it's fitting you should control the world. I don't care if you're a Muslim or a Christian; this beauty is my wife, and henceforth the Great Sultana.

SULTANA.

I am a Christian, so much so that I will not change my faith for a million promises, nor the threat of death. And consider the imprudence of a case so rare that your subjects will perforce judge it as folly. Where, my lord, has anyone seen two in a bed, one who holds Mohammed in his heart, and the other Christ? Your desires do not measure up to your supreme valor, for Love cannot bring together two people divided by their faiths. Stick to your nobility, your rites, and your sect, for it's not right for them to mingle with my faith and my baseness.

TURK.

I enter this debate as Love allows; I am your circumference, and you, my lady, are my center; things between us will be equal, and will never reach a point of inequality. Majesty and Love never go well together—they are only compared so as to praise the greater one. This leads to what you shall see: humbling myself at your feet, I raise you to my head.[20] We are equal now.

---

20. Raising or placing something on one's head was a sign of respect and often used rhetorically, as here. The Spanish custom is of Muslim origin. The phrase occurs often in early modern Spanish usage, as in the famous scrutiny of Don Quixote's library (part 1, ch. 6) and in Calderón's *La cisma de Inglaterra* (The Schism in England), in which a confused Henry VIII mistakes letters from Luther and Pope Leo X and puts the former on his head in an ill-fated mixup.

SULTANA.

Arise, my lord, arise, for such humility amazes me.

MAMÍ.

He has surrendered; he is defeated.

SULTANA.

I ask a favor of you, and you must grant it to me.

TURK.

I obey and do not dispute whatever you might want. Set free, condemn, ransom, absolve, strip away, grant favors, for you can do this
and more, my lady. Love expands your empire. Ask of me whatever
impossibilities desire offers you, for in the hope of being yours, I
believe I shall make them possible. Don't be content with little, my
love; for, though I'm a sinner, I shall work miracles to please you.

SULTANA.

I only ask three days of you, Sultan, to think . . .

TURK.

Three days will kill me.

SULTANA.

. . . about certain doubts of mine, which have made me hesitant,
and, after those three days, you shall come, and you'll see clearly
what you have in my heart.

TURK.

I am content. Go in peace, battle of my thoughts, increase of my
pleasures, solace of my anguish. You two, distressed and happy at
once, shall have your wages increased sixfold. Go, Rustán; tell the
news of my longed-for wedding to all those captive women.

MAMÍ.

You bring them great news!

TURK.

And let them henceforth serve—tell them this as well—and worship my beautiful Catalina as something divine.

[*Exit the* TURK, MAMÍ, *and* RUSTÁN, *and the* SULTANA
remains alone in the theater.]

SULTANA.

I turn to you, oh Lord, who raised Adam from his miserable first
fall with your own life and blood. As he lost us, You redeem us. To

You, blessed shepherd, who sought the one small lost sheep out of a hundred, and, finding it pursued by the wolf, threw it over your holy shoulders, to you I turn in my bitter affliction. You must aid me, Lord: for I am a lamb lost from your fold, and I fear that, sooner or later, if you do not come to my aid, this infernal serpent will catch me!

▦ END OF ACT I ▦

Act II

[*Enter two* MOORS *leading* MADRIGAL, *whose hands are bound behind his back, and with them the* GREAT CADÍ, *who is the bishop and judge of the Turks.*]

FIRST MOOR.

As we told you, by information we obtained, we caught him in fla-
grante committing the great sin. The Arab woman is imprisoned,
and since she knows she has no excuse, she's confessed all her
wrongdoing.

CADÍ.

Throw them into the sea[1] bound hand and foot, with weights to
keep them from swimming. But if he turns Turk, marry them and
set them free.

MADRIGAL.

Brothers, you may tie me up.

CADÍ.

What does the dog choose: marriage or death?

MADRIGAL.

All is death, and all is suffering; I find nothing good in marrying or
in living. If it did not imply leaving the faith through which I hope
to save myself, I would extend my life with marriage, though it too is
death. But marriage and turning Turk are two deaths, so that bound,
I run to my death and freely, I keep my faith. But I know that this
time I shall not die, good sir.

CADÍ.

How, if I sentence you to death, and I am the supreme judge? My
verdicts cannot be appealed.

MADRIGAL.

All in all, I'm content with my fortune, though it is a bad one. I shall

---

1. This was a common punishment for exogamous romance between Muslim women and
Christian men; Madrigal refers to the punishment again later in this act.

soon have the stone around my neck, and you must know that I don't plan to drown. I'll bet on it. And to end your suspense, have these two leave: I'll tell you how it will work.

CADÍ.

Go, and leave him tied up, for I want to see how he escapes the death to which he's condemned.

[*The two* MOORS *exit.*]

MADRIGAL.

You must well remember—for it cannot be otherwise—that wise man named Appolonius of Tyana,[2] who, as you know, either by heaven's favor or by knowledge acquired with time and effort, learned to decipher the songs of birds so well that, when he heard them, said: "This is what they say." And this is true: whether it was the canary who sang, the goldfinch who warbled, the dove who cooed, the crows who cawed, he understood the hidden secrets of birdsong from the malicious sparrow to the imperial eagle. He was, as they say, my ancestor's ancestor, to whom alone he left his talent. Only one learned it out of all those who lived at that time, and only one inherits it from his closest relatives. It has been passed down from one generation to the next, with the strength of time, to be sealed in my unlucky heart.

This morning, when I was going to sin, since my soul has been surrounded by hopes and fears, I heard a little nightingale in a Jew's house, singing this with heavenly harmony: "Where are you going, you wretch? Change your path, and flee from the opportunity that calls and leads you to your end. They will catch you in the noose once you've attained your desire, and without this remedy you will die: tell the judge of your case that the heavens have decreed that he die in six days and descend to the Stygian kingdom; but if he rectifies three great offenses against two Moors and a widow that he committed a few years ago, and if he performs Salat, first washing his body with such and such water (and he said which kind, which I don't want

---

2. Appolonius of Tyana, or Appolonius Tyaneus, was a Pythagorean philosopher writing around the first century A.D. He became a mythical hero, had miracles attributed to him, and was a pagan alternative to Christ among Roman believers.

to tell you), he will have health in body and soul and will be greatly favored by the Great Signor."

Along with this marvelous talent, I have one even greater: I make beasts talk in a very short time. And I offer to teach the Great Signor's huge elephant to speak Turkish clearly within ten years; and if I fail at this, may they impale me, burn me in the fire, and dismember me bit by bit.

CADÍ.

You must tell me about the water, for it's important.

MADRIGAL.

I await its time, for it must be distilled from certain herbs and elderberries. You will not recognize it, but I will; and it must be collected under a clear sky three nights hence.

[*The* CADÍ *unties him*].

CADÍ.

I'm setting you free. But one thing has me puzzled and confused, friend: I don't know which widow it could be, or which Moors I must make amends to: the Moors I offended are countless, and the widows more than a hundred.

MADRIGAL.

I shall go and listen to the nightingale again, and I am certain that his little song will tell me the names of those we don't know.

CADÍ.

I shall tell those Moors why I'm freeing you, which is that you are to make the elephant speak Turkish. But tell me: Do you by chance know Turkish?

MADRIGAL.

By no means!

CADÍ.

Then how can you teach what you don't know?

MADRIGAL.

I'll learn every day what I want to teach it, and ten years will be time enough to learn Turkish, and Greek, too.

CADÍ.

You're right. Know, friend, that I'm putting my life in your hands. The reward for this will be your liberty, at least.

MADRIGAL.

Penitence, great Cadí; penitence and a firm intention not to wrong
the righteous so often from this day forward!

CADÍ.

Don't forget the herbs, for that's the important part of the memora-
ble event you've related, which I believe without a doubt: for I know
that Apollonius of Tyana existed and understood birdsong, and I
also know that there is an art to make mutes speak.

MADRIGAL.

Excellent! I'll await the elephant and have the herbs ready for you.
[*Exeunt. The* TURK *appears behind green taffeta curtains; four
old* PASHAS *enter, who sit on carpets and pillows; enter the Persian*
AMBASSADOR, *and when he comes in they place a brocade over him;
two Turks lead him by the arm, having first checked whether he carries
any concealed weapons; they lead him to sit on a velvet pillow;
the curtain is drawn, and the* TURK *appears.
While this happens, shawms may sound. All being seated,
the* AMBASSADOR *says:*]

AMBASSADOR.

May Allah make your powerful state prosper, universal lord of virtu-
ally the whole earth; may it extend for many centuries, by favorable
luck and heaven's will. I shall relay the embassy of the one who has
sent me (with few preliminaries, as I am wont), if, that is, you grant
me license to speak; for without it I fall silent in your presence.

FIRST PASHA.

Speak briefly, as you have promised, for if you do as you are wont,
the Great Signor will agree to pay you heed, even though we've
forced him to listen to you. After much persuading he has come to
give you an audience and an answer, for he seldom hears out the
enemy. Speak, then; for already you go on too long.

AMBASSADOR.

I speak, then. The Sultan[3] says, my lord, that if you desire peace, he
requests it of you, and asks that it be made with such honest and just

3. Here the ambassador refers to the sultan or shah of Persia, as later in his speech.

laws that time or bitterness will not break them. If to his good soul
you match yours, both of you will reap a heavenly reward.

SECOND PASHA.

Offer no advice; propose, relate your embassy.

AMBASSADOR.

The request for peace has summarized it all.

FIRST PASHA.

That redhead, that wretch, who, with a depraved and barbarous
appetite, follows some of Mohammed's ceremonies and refuses
others—of course he thinks the Great Signor's infinite power, which
awes, grips, and controls the world (may heaven keep him), should
make vile truces. We know your lord's beggary and his tricks, and
thus I make myself his enemy again, given that the great king of
Spain has seen many Persians in his court. These are the deeds of
your lord: to seek favor from one who adores Christ, and when he is
denied, to beg for a cowardly peace with humble pleas.

AMBASSADOR.

That majesty that astonishes and amazes the world; the true por-
trait of Philip the Second, whom only his own Third could follow;
he whose high and mighty power I cannot praise as I would; he,
in sum, upon whose kingdoms the sun endlessly gazes—his name
and virtue, conveyed to my lord the Sultan's ears on the wings of
glorious fame, so inflame his senses with the desire to see him that
he demands, solicits, and requires me to go see the great king on
unknown paths, over strange seas and kingdoms.

FIRST PASHA.

You allow this? Throw him out. Go, flatterer, Christian ambassador.
Throw him out, since nothing good can come of those who profess
his doctrine. Bow your body, and lower your head. Throw him out,
I say.

SECOND PASHA.

Should he not die instead?

FIRST PASHA.

He holds the rank of an ambassador, on whom we cannot carry out
such a verdict.

[*They eject the* AMBASSADOR *with pushes and shoves.*]
It's no surprise, Great Signor, that I become unruly and raise my
voice, aflame with choler, at the great shamelessness of this traitor.
May Your Majesty now consider and declare what response should
be given to this dog.

TURK.

Inform me and advise me as the case requires it. See if the truce is
convenient and honorable.

SECOND PASHA.

From what I can tell, one could not ask for more than a truce in the
east, provided the Persian does not open a front against you. It's a
sad story: Persia does as much harm to us as Flanders does to Spain.[4]
It is right to make peace, for the reasons written on this parchment.

TURK.

You're quick to embrace an idle peace; quick to seek a pleasant
reward. You, brave Braín, do you not oppose Mustafá? Perhaps you
too request the peace?

FIRST PASHA.

I prepare for war, and shall give the reasons in writing.

TURK.

I'll read them and consider what they contain, and shall inform you
of my opinion.

FIRST PASHA.

May Allah, who holds the world in his fingers, give you the richest
and largest part of it.

SECOND PASHA.

May Mohammed thus arrange a fortunate peace so that the sound
of warlike Mars may be heard not in Persia but in Rome, and so that
your galleys may ply the Spanish shores.

[*Exeunt. Enter the* SULTANA *and* RUSTÁN.]

---

4. The Spanish Habsburgs fought a long, drawn-out war (the Eighty Years' War) to retain
control of the Low Countries. Eventually, the Peace of Westphalia in 1648 separated the Prot-
estant northern Netherlands (the United Provinces, later Holland) and the Catholic southern
Flanders (later Belgium).

RUSTÁN.

As though a jewel, he may enjoy you at his pleasure.

SULTANA.

The bold faith of my purpose exceeds all of his might: I'm resolved
to die before I make him happy.

RUSTÁN.

I have nothing to say against such good intentions; but know that
such force can do much, my lady; and consider that he is not persuading or forcing you to turn Turk.

SULTANA.

Is it not a great sin for me to be joined to an infidel?

RUSTÁN.

If you could flee from him, that's what I would have advised; but
when force trumps reason and right, then there is no sin in the
deed if there is none in the intent. Intention saves or damns us in
all we do.

SULTANA.

That's going to extremes.

RUSTÁN.

Yes, but reasonable ones: it's wrong to endanger the soul when its
body is constrained by cords that would overcome a tiger. From this
truth comes one that nobody can deny: the sinner is the one who
compels, not the one compelled.

SULTANA.

I shall be a martyr if I consent to die rather than to sin.

RUSTÁN.

Martyrdom is for a loftier reason: losing one's life for confessing
one's faith.

SULTANA.

I shall take that opportunity.

RUSTÁN.

Who offers it to you? The Sultan loves you as a Christian, and by
force, if not willingly, he can shear the wool without killing the
sheep. Many saints desired martyrdom, and attempted to achieve
it, but that was not enough, for being a martyr requires outstand-

ing virtue. It is an exceptional favor that God grants to whom He
wishes.

SULTANA.

Since I do not deserve so much, I shall beg heaven to grant strength
to my holy purpose; I shall do what I can, and in silence, in my
apprehension, I shall cry out to the heavens.

RUSTÁN.

Quiet, Mamí's coming.

[*Enter* MAMÍ.]

MAMÍ.

The Sultan is coming to see you.

SULTANA.

A deathly sight for me!

MAMÍ.

My lady, you speak amiss.

SULTANA.

I shall always speak thus; and don't try to seem prudent by advising
me.

MAMÍ.

I know you will soon command me, and it's not good to displease you.

[*Enter the* TURK.]

TURK.

Catalina!

SULTANA.

That's my name.

TURK.

They will call you Catalina the Ottoman.

SULTANA.

I am a Christian, and refuse that last name, for mine is de Oviedo, a
noble, renowned, and Christian one.

TURK.

The Ottoman name is not a humble one.

SULTANA.

I grant you that, for none can equal you in arrogance and
haughtiness.

TURK.

Then your name exceeds and surpasses mine in everything, since you scorn the greatest one on earth for its sake!

SULTANA.

It has that within it which I prize, which is to make me known as a Christian when it is called.

TURK.

Your liberties astound me, for they are beyond a woman's; but you may well take them with one who is only capable of what your courage allows him. From that I know that you prize yourself for what you are worth, and with such arrogance you both please and hurt me. Prove yourself more sovereign, make the world respect you, for, indeed, you shall be the Great Sultana. And henceforth I give you that privilege: so be it.

SULTANA.

Would you raise a slave to the excellence of being your wife? Think well on it, for I fear you will soon regret it.

TURK.

I have already considered it, and in this I do nothing extreme, except perhaps to mix Ottoman blood with your Christian blood to make it greater. If the fruit I expect from you comes to pass, the world shall see a firstborn second to none. The sun will not shine in its entire orbit on one who can surpass or equal a Spanish Ottoman. Determine what you will do, Catalina, for my soul already divines that you will bear most beautiful lions.

SULTANA.

I would rather engender eagles.[5]

TURK.

No obstacle can impede your fortune. You are at the top of her wheel, and, though it's unsteady, it will hold still for you, settled in your glory. This afternoon I shall give you possession of my soul, and of my body, which burns in flames of love for you—an inner love, whose powerful force commands my soul and my will.

---

5. The Sultana refers to the imperial eagle, which appears on the Habsburg coat of arms.

SULTANA.

I shall remain a Christian.

TURK.

Be one. For now, my soul adores your body as if it were its very heaven. Am I in charge of your soul, or am I God to sway it, or even lead it to eternal glory? Live as you see fit, so long as you do not live without me.

RUSTÁN.

What do you think, Mamí?

MAMÍ.

A woman can do great things!

SULTANA.

You shall not forbid me to speak with other Christians, my lord.

MAMÍ.

This is nonsense, and to grant it would be even more absurd.

TURK.

As you stand and as I stand, Sultana, you may ask whatever you desire of me with firm and strong dominion. I have given you complete jurisdiction over my will; your desires are my desires: see, then, how obligated I am to fulfill them.

MAMÍ.

A serious case, unprecedented among Turks, to see your Christ roaming around here, Rustán.

RUSTÁN.

He Himself knows it. He makes much good from great evil, Mamí.

TURK.

Order me how to behave so as not to displease you in the slightest; for to know your will, to understand it, and to carry it out will be as one in my soul. Take from this humbleness, most beautiful Catalina, which surrenders its will. I don't want pleasures conquered by the force of overwhelming power; those taken by force are never perfect. As my slave, I could possess you in a minute; but I want to make you my lady, to increase my happiness. And though another's fruit is often sweeter than one's own, how strange!—I long for what is all mine. I hold it in my hands, and in an instant it is gone. Oh empty fears, how low I have fallen! I can satisfy my desire and I linger on courtesies.

RUSTÁN.

Humble your thoughts, for the Great Signor seems to me quite incensed. Don't summon your sorrow in his anger; you should not beseech one whom you can command.

SULTANA.

Fear brought low my holy zeal. O tender age! How easily any worry defeats you! Great Signor, you see me here; I bend my knees before you; I am your slave.

TURK.

How now? Raise your face, my lady, and in those two suns that so beautify it you will make my eyes see the great power of God, or of nature, to whom Allah gave the power to work miracles with its beauty.

SULTANA.

Be warned that I am a Christian and always shall be.

MAMÍ.

A strange and wondrous case: a Christian Great Sultana!

TURK.

You can make laws for the world and keep the faith you choose: you're not mine but your own. Your worth beyond compare demands not just human respect but adoration, and thus I promise to fulfill the very shadow of your intent. Mamí, bring me—on your life—the captives from the seraglio so that they may vow their obedience to the Sultana.

[*Exit* MAMÍ.]

Not only those who owe me obedience shall revere her, but all peoples from this pole to the other.

SULTANA.

My lord, your desires go beyond what is meet!

TURK.

The things that please me are neither measured nor rated; they are all extreme, and to achieve them, I always hope and never fear.

[MAMÍ *returns, and with him come* CLARA, *called* ZAIDA, *and* ZELINDA, *who is* LAMBERTO, *whom* ROBERTO *seeks.*]

MAMÍ.

Here they are.

TURK.

Let these two swear obedience for all of them.

ZAIDA.

May God bless your nuptials and make them joyous; may your womb be fertile, and may the Great Sultan's state see the timely birth of an heir; may you achieve your aims, for I know them from Rustán; and may the world give you its blessings in a thousand ways.

ZELINDA.

Most beautiful Spaniard, crown of her nation, discreet like no other, and singular in good intentions; may heaven bring your wishes to fruition, for it knows them well; and may the pious and sweet Hymenaeus[6] revel in these nuptials; let the empire you possess be ruled by your judgment; and may you desire nothing that you do not achieve. Clearly Mohammed himself exalts you!

TURK.

Do not name Mohammed to her, for the Sultana is a Christian. Her name is Doña Catalina, and her last name, de Oviedo—to my advantage, since if it were Moorish, she would never have come into my power, nor would I enjoy the treasure that is her beauty. And now, with no silence to disguise it, I worship the great name of my comely Catalina as something divine. To celebrate the nuptials, which will astound the world, may heaven grant me its glory and may all my people attend; let the deep sea bestow on me its tastiest fish from its frightful depths; may land and sky grant me game and birds, such that each may make the choicest dish.

SULTANA.

My lord, I do not warrant the praises you sing of me.

TURK.

For your crowns, let the south grant me its pearls and Arabia its gold, Tyre its purple and Sheba its fragrances. Let April and May give flowers to adorn your forehead. And if you think my requests make little sense, come and you shall see it all.

---

6. Hymenaeus, or Hymen, was the Greek god of marriage and commonly invoked in Renaissance texts that celebrated it.

[*Exeunt all but* ZAIDA *and* ZELINDA.]

ZELINDA.

Oh Clara! How dim our prospects look! What will we do? We're
already at our wit's end! I, a man, and in the Sultan's seraglio? I can't
imagine any path, remedy, or plan to get out of this.

ZAIDA.

Nor can I. Great was your daring!

ZELINDA.

It followed Love, who ignores fear when it seeks its happiness. Skirt-
ing death on every side, I would come to see you, my love, amid
blades of steel unsheathed against me. I have seen you and possessed
you, and whatever ill (though mortal) may follow cannot equal this
boon.

ZAIDA.

You speak like a lover: you're all verve, valor, and hope, but our misfortune has no possible remedy. Death is the only way out of this sad
place, which it was our misfortune to enter. There's no fleeing from
here to a safer place: one can only escape on the wings of death. No
bribe is enough to soften the guards, nor is there any solution that
avoids death. I, pregnant, and you, a man, and in this seraglio? Death
has us in its sights.

ZELINDA.

Enough! Since our fortunes must end in death, we must not hope
for an escape; but know, Clara, that we must die in such a way that
death attains for us a new and everlasting life. I mean that we should
die as Christians no matter what happens.

ZAIDA.

I care not for life so long as we rush to such a death.

[*Exeunt. Enter* MADRIGAL, *the elephant's teacher, with a small tin*
trumpet, and with him ANDREA, *the spy.*]

ANDREA.

Madrigal, I told you that the Arab woman would be the death of you
one day!

MADRIGAL.

She did me more good than ill.

ANDREA.

She made you an elephant's teacher.

MADRIGAL.

Isn't it something, Andrea? No one will ever see anything like it.

ANDREA.

Won't you die in the end, when they figure out the trick?

MADRIGAL.

That doesn't matter. Let me live for now, for in ten years' time the elephant, the Sultan, or I will die, which will remedy my woes. Wouldn't it have been worse to let them throw me into the ocean tied up in a sack where I could drown, without the aid of my great swimming abilities? Aren't I better off now? Can't you help me now, for both our sakes?

ANDREA.

That's true.

MADRIGAL.

Andrea, this is a great feat, and I intend to get away with it when you least expect it.

ANDREA.

You have talents, Madrigal, which I commend to the devil. Will the elephant speak?

MADRIGAL.

It won't lack a teacher, and it's such an able beast, I think it must have a certain something of rational discourse.

ANDREA.

Clearly you are the animal devoid of reason. The nonsense you hit upon is unlike anything any rational person would find.

MADRIGAL.

It's good to make the Cadí think so.

ANDREA.

You're doing well; but don't try to compete with me, for that's wrong.

MADRIGAL.

My nature is to make fun of my closest friends.

ANDREA.

Is that a silver trumpet?

MADRIGAL.

I requested a silver one, but the person who gave it to me said that tin was good enough. I must speak into the elephant's ear with it.

ANDREA.

A waste of time and effort!

MADRIGAL.

A great plan and a beautiful trick! They give me a stipend of one hundred ásperos[7] a day.

ANDREA.

Two escudos? What a tale! Your trickery is going well!

MADRIGAL.

Here's the Cadí. Till later—I have to speak with him.

ANDREA.

Will you try to trick him again?

MADRIGAL.

Perhaps I might.

[*Exit* ANDREA, *and enter the* CADÍ.]

CADÍ.

Spaniard, have you begun instructing the elephant?

MADRIGAL.

Yes, and it's making good progress: I've given it four lessons.

CADÍ.

In what language?

MADRIGAL.

In Basque, which is the language that plainly takes the prize for being older than Ethiopian and Abyssinian.

CADÍ.

It seems a strange tongue to me. Where is it spoken?

MADRIGAL.

In Vizcaya.[8]

CADÍ.

And Vizcaya is . . . ?

7. See the Introduction for a discussion of coinage.

8. Vizcaya, or Biscay, is the Basque region of Spain. The Basque language—a pre-Indo-European tongue—is not related to Indo-European languages spoken near it, such as Spanish, French, and Catalan.

MADRIGAL.

There on the border of Navarre, next to Spain.

CADÍ.

This powerful language is unique in its antiquity; teach it Spanish, which we understand better.

MADRIGAL.

I'll teach him all the grave languages I know, and he'll take what he wants.

CADÍ.

And which ones do you know?

MADRIGAL.

The argot of blind men, the Italian *bergamasca*, Gallic Gascon, and ancient Greek;[9] I'll make him a primer with letters from the press so that he can get the famous cant. And if he doesn't like these, for they're somewhat rocky, I'll teach him the mellifluous Valencian and Portuguese.

CADÍ.

Your life risks grave danger if the elephant does not become a great student of Turkish, Moorish, or at least Spanish.

MADRIGAL.

It will be well versed in all of them, if it pleases the infinite provider to good men, and even to bad men, for He makes the sun shine on them all.

CADÍ.

Do me a favor, Spaniard.

MADRIGAL.

Certainly, I'll be glad to. State your will, and I shall do as you say.

CADÍ.

It will be the greatest your friendship can offer me. Tell me: What were those crows you saw flying today talking about in their coarse and sad voice? Because I couldn't ask you then.

---

9. The *bergamasca* (bergomask in English) was a lusty sixteenth-century dance depicting the reputedly awkward manners of the inhabitants of Bergamo, in northern Italy, where it supposedly originated. Gallic Gascon: a dialect of Gascony in France.

MADRIGAL.

You must know—and you must not doubt what you'll hear from me—you must know, I say, that they were speaking of going to the fields of Alcudia,[10] where they could satisfy their great hunger: for there's always a dead cow in those wide fields on which to fill their bellies.

CADÍ.

Where are those fields?

MADRIGAL.

In Spain.

CADÍ.

Quite a trip!

MADRIGAL.

Crows fly so fast that they cover a thousand leagues in a trice: they fly so hard that today they awaken in France, and go to sleep in Paris.

CADÍ.

Tell me: What was that goldfinch saying yesterday?

MADRIGAL.

I couldn't make it out— it's Hungarian, I don't understand it.

CADÍ.

And that pretty lark, did you catch what it was saying?

MADRIGAL.

Some nonsense that you don't need to know.

CADÍ.

I know you'll tell me.

MADRIGAL.

She said, in sum, that you were after a garzon, and some other little things.

CADÍ.

May Lucifer take her! Why does she meddle with me?

MADRIGAL.

If there's something to it, you can tell that I understand her.

---

10. Alcudia: a town in Extremadura where cattle are taken for winter grazing (Covarrubias 78).

CADÍ.

She's not too far off; but I'm not yet burning in such a fire. Don't tell anyone a thing, for my reputation would be ruined.

MADRIGAL.

My tongue is mute to reproach you. You can rest easy in my confidence, for I'm determined always to speak your praises. Even if the thrushes proclaim your vileness, and the finches that chirp in the buds speak of it; whether the asses bray to tell of your perverse deeds, or the crows caw or the canaries sing—since I'm the only one who understands them, I'll be the one to silence them from one pole to the other.

CADÍ.

Is there no bird that sings of my virtue?

MADRIGAL.

They will respect you from here on, O Cadí! if I can do anything about it. As soon as I see a sign on their lips of your failings, I shall cut out their tongues to punish them for offending you.

[Enter RUSTÁN, the eunuch, and behind him an old CAPTIVE who listens to what they are saying.]

CADÍ.

Good Rustán, where are you going?

RUSTÁN.

To find a Spanish tarasí.

MADRIGAL.

Isn't that a tailor?

RUSTÁN.

Yes.

MADRIGAL.

Then you're looking for me, for I'm Spanish and a tailor, with such large scissors that the sun's great tailor doesn't have the like in his sphere. What are we to cut?

RUSTÁN.

Rich garments for the Sultana, who dresses in the Christian fashion.

CADÍ.

Have you lost your senses? Rustán, what are you saying? There's a Sultana, and she dresses in the Christian fashion?

RUSTÁN.

It's no joke; you heard the truth. Her name is Doña Catalina, her last name de Oviedo.

CADÍ.

You must be telling some tale to awe and anger me.

RUSTÁN.

The Sultan has married a beautiful captive, and by his love he allows her to live in the Christian faith, and to dress and behave as a Christian, as she pleases.

CAPTIVE.

O holy and just heaven!

CADÍ.

Have you ever heard such nonsense? I'll die if I don't go and scold him right away.

[Exit the CADÍ.*]*

RUSTÁN.

You'll go in vain, since you'll find him all ablaze with love. Come with me, and make sure you're a good tailor.

MADRIGAL.

Sir, there's none better in this great city, neither captive nor renegade; and to prove it, know that I am the one named to teach the elephant; and one who is to make a beast speak must be elegant at making clothes.

RUSTÁN.

I think you're right; but if you don't give me another reason, I'm against you from now on. Yet all in all I'll take you. Come on.

CHRISTIAN.[11]

Sir, if you please, I would speak with you alone.

RUSTÁN.

Speak, for I shall hear you.

CHRISTIAN.

It's clear to me from several things that this fellow knows little or

---

11. This character is the same as the old CAPTIVE given in the list of dramatis personae. There is no evidence in the play that this character is any more a tailor than Madrigal is, though he may be more familiar with court manners. If he is a poor nobleman, as he claims elsewhere, he is adopting the same ruse in order to approach Catalina.

nothing of the tailor's art; I am a court tailor, and from Spain, at least, and one of the best there at cutting and fitting. In sum, I am a ladies' tailor, and have become a captive mysteriously, perhaps, but no doubt tragically. Take me with you: you may see marvels.

RUSTÁN.

All right. Come, then, and you too; one of you will get it right.

MADRIGAL.

Friend, are you a tailor?

CHRISTIAN.

Yes.

MADRIGAL.

Well, I commend myself to Judas if I know how to sew a patch.

CHRISTIAN.

What a great tailor! Even so, I shall cut some snippets from this—by skill rather than by force—that will carry me back to Spain.

[*Exeunt omnes. Enter the* SULTANA *with a rosary in hand, and the* TURK *behind her, listening to her.*]

SULTANA.

Virgin more beautiful than the sun; Mother of God, whom the greatest praise; guiding star through the sea of the world, who shows the soul the reward for its storms! I invoke you in my affliction; I am drowning, O great Lady, now I drift onto the shoals of weak and blind fear, to which I hand over my anxious soul. I offer you my will, which is mine and which I preserve, most holy Mary; see how I faint; grant me, Lady, the good that I do not deserve.[12]
O Great Signor! You here?

TURK.

Pray, Catalina, pray, for without divine aid human things do not last; and call on your Lela Marién,[13] for it doesn't frighten me, on the contrary, it seems good to me, for she is sainted among us as well.

---

12. This type of affective language was fairly common in Spanish Marian devotion. One of the Virgin's titles is Star of the Sea (Stella Maris). Less common is Spouse of your Son (*esposa de tu Hijo*), though many litanies refer to Mary as the spouse of the Holy Spirit (and thus technically of Christ). In Counter-Reformation Spain there was also a tradition of viewing Mary as coparticipant in the Passion. See Boon.

13. Lela Marién: Arabic title of Mary, as with Zara in *The Bagnios of Algiers,* though the Arabic denies her virginity; literally, "Lady Mary."

SULTANA.

There is no nation that does not bless you, O Spouse of your Son!
O more beautiful than the moon!

TURK.

You can praise her as you like, for we do the same, and we honor her
above all for her virginity.

[*Enter* RUSTÁN, MADRIGAL, *the old* CAPTIVE *and* MAMÍ.]

RUSTÁN.

Here are the tailors.

MADRIGAL.

I, my lord, am the one who knows all that befits the office; the others
are imposters.

SULTANA.

You will dress me in the Spanish fashion.

MADRIGAL.

I'll gladly do that, so long as there's a little something for the
chirinola.

SULTANA.

What is a *chirinola*?

MADRIGAL.

A dress designed in such a fashion that no queen has ever worn one
so beautiful; it takes three hundred yards of gold and silver fabric.

SULTANA.

Then who could walk in it without becoming exhausted?

MADRIGAL.

The skirt, my lady, will be false.

CHRISTIAN.

Well! This man is out of his mind, or jests, or babbles. Friend, your
jests are very poor, and know, if you don't already, that with such
important people jokes never go over well. I'll make you a suitable
dress in the Spanish fashion.

SULTANA.

Unless his voice deceives me, this man is surely my father. Take my
measurements, good man.

CAPTIVE.

The heavens should have taken the measure of your life!

SULTANA.

There's no doubt, it's him. What shall I do? I'm bewildered!

TURK.

I'll reward you with your liberty and great wealth. Dress her for me in the Spanish fashion, with garments so lovely that their opulence awes, just as she, unrivaled, awes; use Oriental pearls and Indian diamonds, for I shall easily place in your hands whatever you might desire. Let my Catalina be seen adorned as she wishes, for to me she will be divine in whatever she wears.

CAPTIVE.

Come here, precious jewel; I shall take your measurements, though they should be the measure of your funeral shroud.

MADRIGAL.

He begins at the waist—he's as much a tailor as I am.

TURK.

Christian friend, not that—that's a bit shameless; size her up from afar, and don't touch her.

CAPTIVE.

Where, my lord, has anyone seen a tailor work like that? Don't you see that I would get the cut wrong if I didn't have the measurements as a guide?

TURK.

That's true; but I would prefer it if we could avoid it.

CAPTIVE.

There's nothing to fear from my embraces, my lord, for the Sultana can receive them as though a father's.

SULTANA.

My suspicion is confirmed; now my fear exceeds anything I've felt so far.

TURK.

Come close and do your work.

SULTANA.

Good father, don't give signs of being anything but a tailor.

[*As he takes her measurements, the* FATHER *says:*]

CAPTIVE.

Would to God that these laces that make up your dress were for carrying you to the grave in my arms! Would to God that the greatness of this majesty were instead humbleness in your land, and that these rich adornments were rough woolen cloth, enjoyed in Spain behind nets and lathes!

SULTANA.

No more, father, for I can't suffer these rebukes; my heart fails me and I faint away!

[*The* SULTANA *faints.*]

TURK.

What is this? What confusion is this? What desperation? Tell me, enchanter, impostor: Have you bewitched her? Have you killed her? Tell me, basilisk: What have you done? Speak, evil spirit.

CAPTIVE.

She will soon recover. Have them loosen her bodice, and splash her face with water, and you'll see how she comes to her senses.

TURK.

Her life slips away! Impale this monster straightaway! Impale that one too! Take them from my sight!

MADRIGAL.

And so I die before the elephant!

MAMÍ.

Come, dog!

CAPTIVE.

I am the father of the Sultana, who lives.

MAMÍ.

One whom the truth doesn't avail falls back on lies. Come on, impostors, arrogant Spaniards.

MADRIGAL.

O flower of all elephants! Today I delay in coming to you.

[MAMÍ *and* RUSTÁN *carry* MADRIGAL *and the* SULTANA'S FATHER *out by force; the* TURK *remains on stage with the* SULTANA, *still unconscious.*]

TURK.

You shall come on my shoulders, o heaven to this poor Atlas,
unmatched in my grief, if you don't come to your senses!
[*He carries her off.*]

◈   END OF ACT II   ◈

Act III

[*Enter* RUSTÁN *and* MAMÍ.]

MAMÍ.

Had the Sultana not recovered so quickly from her grave convulsion, she would have been left fatherless, and the elephant teacherless. She awoke, and loudly said: "What happened to my father? Woe is me! Where is my father?" her eyes searching all around for him. Without waiting for answers to such belated questions, the Great Signor ordered me to go remove the two *tarasíes* from the stake or the fire, guessing most exactly that the elder was the beloved father of his dearest jewel. I rushed to them and found them when the executioner was already sharpening the tips of the stakes on which they would be tortured. The Spanish teacher had barely been freed when he skipped twice and said "Thanks be to God and to my disciple!"; convinced, I think, that they were freeing him so he could make the elephant speak, as he has promised. I brought the aged father before the Great Sultana, who received him with tender embraces, kissing him a thousand times. There they briefly told each other a thousand various things that had happened to them. Finally, the Great Signor ordered me to arrange lodging for his father-in-law in the Jewish quarter.[1] He commands that he be served in the Christian fashion, with the pomp and ceremony that his love and greatness call for.

RUSTÁN.

This is a strange case! He loves her tenderly; his will is ruled by the Christian's. He paid no heed to the great Cadí, suspecting that he would condemn his intentions with heavy reprimands. Two days hence, the Great Signor wants to enjoy Christian dances in the sera-

---

1. In Cervantes's time, there were several areas settled by Jews in Istanbul. Cervantes here may mean the area now at the foot of the Galata Bridge where the imperial Ottoman Mosque Yeni Cami stands. This mosque, built by the historical sultana, was located in a mainly Jewish neighborhood near the palace until the quarter was cleared so that the mosque could be built around 1660. See Shaw 49–51.

glio with the Sultana and his captive women. I've found musicians, Spanish captives, to celebrate—something never seen in the seraglio. Shall I send them clean and dressed in new garments?

MAMÍ.

Yes, but as slaves.

RUSTÁN.

If time allowed, it would be better for them to go as freedmen, with feathers and finery, just like the dances they have in Spain.

MAMÍ.

Don't worry about that; you know it's impossible.

RUSTÁN.

The Sultana already has a Spanish dress.

MAMÍ.

Who made it for her?

RUSTÁN.

A Jew brought it from Algiers, where two roving galleys arrived, their dinghies full of loot. That's where the Jew bought the dress I mentioned.

MAMÍ.

It will be a great indecency for the Sultana to wear another's clothes.

RUSTÁN.

She so longs to take off Turkish dress that I imagine she'd wear serge and sackcloth, so long as the dress were cut in the Christian fashion.

MAMÍ.

I don't care if she wears palmetto leaves or green dock.

RUSTÁN.

Mamí, leave me be, for I have a thousand things to do.

MAMÍ.

And I two thousand and more for Signor Oviedo.

[*Exeunt. Enter the* SULTANA *and her* FATHER, *dressed in black.*]

FATHER.

Daughter, despite all your arguments, it still seems to me that you've come to be who you are by your own faults; I mean, by your pleasure; for if you had more Christian leanings, this tyrant would not enjoy something so unjust. What signs of whipping do your feet and arms show? What ties or binds have cruelly held you down? You've surrendered of your own volition, swayed by this licentious life, this pomp and majesty.

SULTANA.

If I have peacefully assented to this unbeliever, this minister of my torment, may all heaven destroy me, and may your blessing become a curse to me, for my perdition. A thousand times I resolved to die before pleasing him; a thousand times, to anger him, I disdained his courtesies; but all of my disdain, my scorn, and arrogance just made him hold me in higher esteem. My zeal excited him, my disdain attracted him, and my haughtiness brought him closer when I fled him the most. Finally, to keep a Christian name, rather than that of Sultana, I fearfully gave in.

FATHER.

You must realize, to your disadvantage, that you are in a state of mortal sin, my daughter. Look to your state, and to how you conduct yourself, for it is full of troubles, thought it might seem good.

SULTANA.

Since you know how to advise me, tell me, though it's nonsense: is it right for me to kill myself, since they won't kill me? Must I die by my own hand? If He does not wish me to live, does He require me to kill myself by choice or by force?

FATHER.

Desperation[2] is a sin so evil and ugly that no other compares to it, I think. Killing oneself is cowardly and holds back the generous hand of the Sovereign Good that sustains and nourishes us. This great truth is evident from a case beyond doubt: Judas sinned more in hanging himself than in selling Christ.

SULTANA.

I would wish to be a martyr. Though my fragile and sick flesh may slumber at this cursed task for now, I trust that the light that guides the greatest sinner to heaven shall shine brightly on my darkness one day, and take me, repentant, from this captivity where I reign aggrieved to eternal liberty.

---

2. *Desesperación* (desperation, hopelessness) denotes suicide. See note 9 to Act I of *The Bagnios of Algiers*.

FATHER.

Hope, not fear, is what I advise, for the highest power of God cannot be reduced. Confidence in Him, I find, is the way out of this maze; but should it be by death instead, don't run from it, be steadfast.

SULTANA.

May heaven uphold my intentions in my ill fortune, so that, facing this unimagined ordeal, I may repay Him, and satisfy you, father. I must go now, for this afternoon I have much to do; the Great Signor wants to show off my graces. Should you wish to be there, father, it is in your hands.

FATHER.

How could one find himself there who is lost here? Keep your pleasures honest, and do what you know happily and quickly; show yourself to be well raised and well born.

SULTANA.

I shall, though I'm sure that I know little or nothing of graces.

FATHER.

May God keep you in his hand! Go to him, my beloved, well served and dissatisfied. I'm sad and happy in vain!

[*They exit, and the* SULTANA *must dress in the Christian fashion, as elegantly as possible. Enter two* MUSICIANS, *and* MADRIGAL *with them, dressed as captives, with their red jackets, white canvas breeches, black laced borceguíes,*[3] *all new, and collars with no ruff.* MADRIGAL *should carry a small hand drum, and the others their guitars. The* MUSICIANS *are called* FIRST *and* SECOND MUSICIAN.]

FIRST MUSICIAN.

This is another story from being at the foot of the stake, waiting for the lark, that had you out of sorts.

MADRIGAL.

By Holy Christ, I was annoyed! They had gotten half a mast ready, to be a spit for my entrails.

---

3. Although the play presents them as Moorish, these are in fact standard Spanish boots. The term appears in Don Quixote's etymological excursus on Spanish words originally from Arabic in part 2, chapter 67.

SECOND MUSICIAN.

Who made you be a tailor?

MADRIGAL.

The same one who makes us all now poets, musicians, and dancers: the devil, I believe, and no other.

FIRST MUSICIAN.

If the Great Sultana hadn't come to her senses so quickly, you'd be done for!

MADRIGAL.

Like a roast rabbit, minus the grill. Look at this tyrant!

SECOND MUSICIAN.

Be quiet. God grant you a bad Easter! Don't you remember that proverb, "The walls have ears?"

MADRIGAL.

I'll be quiet, and I say . . .

FIRST MUSICIAN.

What? Don't say anything!

MADRIGAL.

I say the Great Signor has his whims, like any other king of his standing, and I fear that any false step we make in the dance will see us basted with lard.[4]

SECOND MUSICIAN.

And do you know how to dance?

MADRIGAL.

Like a mule; but I have a lively ballad that I plan to sing in a mad fashion, and which tells *ad longum* the whole great story of the Great Sultana Catalina.

FIRST MUSICIAN.

How do you know it?

MADRIGAL.

Her father himself told me everything *ad pedem literae*.[5]

---

4. This punishment consisted of dropping burning fat on wounds made with a whip on the victim's back; it was often used in Spain, as with the father of the *pícaro* Lazarillo de Tormes in the eponymous novel. See La Du.

5. Latin, "to the letter."

SECOND MUSICIAN.

What else shall we sing?

MADRIGAL.

A thousand sarabands,[6] a thousand pretty *zambapalos*, a thousand *chaconas*, a thousand *pésame dello*, and a thousand *folías*.

FIRST MUSICIAN.

Who shall dance them?

MADRIGAL.

The Great Sultana.

SECOND MUSICIAN.

It's impossible for her to know any dances, for they say she lost her liberty at a young age.

MADRIGAL.

Look, Capacho, Spanish women are born dancers straight from their mothers' wombs.

FIRST MUSICIAN.

That's true and I won't deny it, but I doubt the Sultana will dance, to keep her decorum.

SECOND MUSICIAN.

Queens also dance at balls.

MADRIGAL.

True; and when they're alone ladies are unreserved, while keeping their honesty.

FIRST MUSICIAN.

If they'd given us some time to meet and decide, perhaps we could have planned a happy dance, set to song as they do for the plays I saw in Spain.[7] Alonso Martínez,[8] God be with him, first invented these dances, which both entertain and delight, more than an interlude of a hungry man, a thief, or a man beaten up.[9]

6. A slow Spanish waltz. The dances described here were racy and often censored in Spain at the time.

7. Spanish drama in the period began with a prologue. This was followed by the play itself, interspersed with shorter plays (interludes) between acts. Finally, a dance concluded the performance.

8. A contemporary actor who worked in several companies.

9. Interludes such as this were made popular by Lope de Rueda, whose *pasos*, or skits, dealt with such humorous topics.

SECOND MUSICIAN.

That's the plain truth.

MADRIGAL.

This time they'll impale us; this time we'll be food for tunas and minnows.

FIRST MUSICIAN.

Madrigal, this is great cowardice; may you always be a false diviner.

[*Enter* RUSTÁN.]

RUSTÁN.

Are you all here, friends?

MADRIGAL.

We're all here, as you see, with our instruments; but so frightened that I fear we'll smell awful in a minute.

RUSTÁN.

You're all clean and well dressed in new clothes; fear not, and come, for the Great Signor awaits you.

MADRIGAL.

I swear on my sins that I'm coming. May God be with me!

SECOND MUSICIAN.

Fear not, for you're scaring us for no reason, and fortune favors the brave.

[*Exeunt. Enter* MAMÍ *to set up a dais, with two or three other* GARZONS; *they unroll a Turkish rug, with five or six colored velvet pillows.*]

MAMÍ.

Pull more on that side, Muza, pull; you go for the cushions, Arnaute; and you, Bairán, see that the flowers are scattered wherever the Great Signor steps, and light the incense. To it, let's finish up!

[*The* GARZONS *do all this without replying, and when the dais is set up, the* TURK *enters, with* RUSTÁN, *the* MUSICIANS, *and* MADRIGAL.]

TURK.

Are you Spaniards, by chance?

MADRIGAL.

We are.

TURK.

From Aragon or Andalusia?

MADRIGAL.

Castilians.

TURK.

Soldiers or skilled workers?

MADRIGAL.

Skilled workers.

TURK.

What's your office?

MADRIGAL.

Mine? Town crier.

TURK.

And what is this fellow's office?

MADRIGAL.

He's a guitarist; I mean that he plays the guitar eighty times worse than his mother.

TURK.

What skill does this other one have?

MADRIGAL.

A great one; he sews sacks and cuts gloves.

TURK.

In truth, those are valuable offices!

MADRIGAL.

My lord, would you rather this one were a smith, the other a shipbuilder, the third a gunpowder expert, or at least a master in artillery?

TURK.

If that were so, I'd prize and reward you above all my other captives.

MADRIGAL.

Well, and there would go our hopes of freedom.

TURK.

When Allah pleases, he makes one man a captive, another free: no one can oppose His will. See whether Catalina comes.

RUSTÁN.

She's coming, and wherever she sets her pretty foot a carnation or a lily blooms.

[*Enter the* SULTANA, *dressed in the Christian fashion, as I've already said, as richly as possible; she wears a small ebony cross on her neck;* ZAIDA *and* ZELINDA *enter with her, who are* CLARA *and* LAMBERTO, *and the three* GARZONS *that set up the dais.*]

TURK.

Welcome, goddess in human form; in truth, more beautiful than the heavens, that center where my heart rests, lives, and delights; more fresh in my eyes than a cool April morn, when, in Dawn's arms, it shines, enamels, embroiders, and gilds the countryside and flatters the world. You don't need to change clothes for the entire world to gladly vow obedience to you.

SULTANA.

I fear so many praises will only serve to insult me, for flattery never says what the soul feels, and thus lies when it praises.

MADRIGAL.

A slap for every lie.

SECOND MUSICIAN.

Madrigal, friend, watch where we are; don't court our death with your tongue.

TURK.

Your worth raises you above the heavens. Come, my lady, and be seated, o sweet end of my troubles, for today my soul will be all eyes, to behold you at its pleasure.

[*The* TURK *and the* SULTANA *sit on the pillows;* RUSTÁN, MAMÍ, *and the* MUSICIANS *remain standing.*]

MAMÍ.

The Cadí is at the door.

TURK.

Open it, and let him in, Mamí, for he should not be turned away. This visit vexes me, the more so here. He must be coming to reproach me, claiming that I am as docile in obeying as I am powerful in commanding. He'll reproach in vain, for Love, whose deeds I praise, has enslaved me and does not allow me to rule.

[*Enter the* CADÍ.]

CADÍ.

What is this I see? Oh no! Heavens, that you should consent to this!

TURK.

On your life, great Cadí, don't reproach me, and sit down here next
to me! Rebukes call for another time and place.

CADÍ.

The quiet you command silences my speech. I will hush and be
seated.

TURK.

Do so. [*To* MUSICIANS:] And you, see that you give me pleasure, as
I've requested, and I will show my gratitude to all.

MADRIGAL.

Before we come to the critical moment of the unlearned dance, hear
a ballad, my lord.

FIRST MUSICIAN.

Please God that this sinner doesn't sink us with this episode!

MADRIGAL.

And you must know that it tells the life of your jewel; and I'll sing
it readily, for there's no one like me for it, and I know it well by
heart.[10]

"A certain So-and-so from Oviedo embarked one winter from
Málaga for Orán on a ship of ten oars. He was a gentleman, but
not a rich one: that's the curse of our times, for it seems that being
poor and being an *hidalgo* are one and the same thing.[11] His wife
and daughter, young and extremely beautiful, went with him
too. The sea promised a fast crossing, as it was January, the time
when corsairs retire to their ports; but since misfortunes sail in all
weather, such a grave one befell them that they lost their liberty.
Morato Arráez,[12] who doesn't sleep in order to keep us from rest,
caught up with the light ship in that crossing; he stopped in Tetuán
and sold the girl straightaway to a famous and rich Moor named Alí
Izquierdo.

---

10. The ballad form Madrigal sings in here was typically used in poetry and theater to provide longer narrative accounts, often a "backstory," as here.

11. Poor *hidalgos*—lesser nobles—were often portrayed in Spanish literature as layabouts
too poor to eat but too proud to work. Perhaps the most famous *hidalgo* of all is Don Quixote.

12. See Act I, note 11.

"The girl's mother died of grief; they brought her father to Algiers, where his old age saved him from rowing in the galleys. Four years had passed when Morato, back in Tetuán, beheld the girl, more lovely than the sun itself. He bought her from his patron, paying Alí eight times what he had paid for her in the first place. Alí told Morato: 'I'm happy to sell her, for I can't turn her Turk with gifts or with pleas. She's only ten years old, but so wise in her years that they trump old men's mature ones. She's the glory of her nation and an exemplar of fortitude, all the more so as she's alone, and of the lesser and fragile sex.' The great corsair, overjoyed with his purchase, came to Constantinople in the year 1600, I believe; he presented her to the Great Signor, a young lad at the time, who immediately handed her over to the eunuchs of the seraglio. They tried to change her sweet name, Catalina, to Zoraida; but she never consented, nor her last name, de Oviedo. Finally, after some time the Great Signor saw her, and as if beholding the sun, was rendered lifeless and amazed; he offered her the inheritance of his extensive kingdoms, and gave her his soul as a sign. . . ."

TURK.

How right he is in that!

MADRIGAL.

"He allows her to be a Christian. . . ."

CADÍ.

A strange concession!

TURK.

Quiet, my friend; don't disturb me, for I'm hearing about my good fortune.

MADRIGAL.

"I don't intend to tell here how her father failed to find her: it would make for a long tale, and if I have to make a long story short, suffice it to say that he came to find her through roundabout wanderings worthy of a longer story, in another time and place. Today Catalina is the Sultana, today she is the queen, she lives today and treads on the Ottoman lion's indomitable neck. Today she defeats and overcomes him, and going to unprecedented lengths, she gives aid to Christians. And that's what I know of these events."

SECOND MUSICIAN.

Oh sudden poet! The fair lord of Delos grant you a draught of Aganippe's water.[13]

FIRST MUSICIAN.

May the Muses prime your palate with ham and aged wine from Rute and Ciudad Real.

MADRIGAL.

I'd be happy with wine from San Martín.[14]

CADÍ.

This Christian is the very devil! I know him well, and I'm certain he knows more than Mohammed.

TURK.

I plan to favor him.

MADRIGAL.

You, my lady, approach in our fashion, for you must be first and last in a dance.

SULTANA.

This won't please the Great Signor, for as I lost my liberty so young I don't know any curious dances.

MADRIGAL.

I shall guide you, my lady.

SULTANA.

Go ahead and begin.

[*The* SULTANA *rises to dance, and she successfully attempts this one.
The* MUSICIANS *sing:*]

[MUSICIANS].

To you, beautiful Spaniard, I hand over my soul. I don't seek my own pleasure; I only seek yours; for you, proud and happy, I go to such lengths that I'd rather be your slave than command a thousand empires; for you, with a clear mind, I won't admit reproaches or hear serious advice, although I well could; for you, against my Prophet, whose precepts command me to hate Christians, for you, I do not

13. Apollo, who was born on the island of Delos, is the god of poetry. Aganippe is the font of Parnassus on Mount Helicon, where the Muses reside.

14. These three cities were famous for their wines.

hate them; with you, apple of my eye, I envision my good fortune, and I know that, without a doubt, I live and die for you.

[*The dance changes.*]

The girl heard the sweet wooing, and her soul cannot find happiness. As she intends to keep her faith, the king's wooing does not please. She turns her thoughts to higher things, without base love disturbing her calm. And her soul cannot find happiness. Her grace and verve are such that they hold the Turk's will captive. He burns with her coolness, her valor astounds him, and he adores her very shadow, although he sees clearly her soul cannot find happiness.

TURK.

Stop, my darling, no more, for you tear my soul out after your every step. May your grace, vivacity, and rhythm give you the prize. Be still, my love, and rest if you're tired; and on this happy day, my generous hand grants liberty to all.

[*When the* TURK *says this, everyone kneels down before him. the* CAPTIVES, *and* ZAIDA *and* ZELINDA, *the* GARZONS *and the* SULTANA.]

SULTANA.

I kiss your feet a thousand times!

ZELINDA.

This has been a most happy outcome for me!

TURK.

Catalina, are you well?

SULTANA.

No, my lord, I admit it; with the great happiness of this highest courtesy that you've shown us, I am dazed.

TURK.

Arise, my lady, for the favor I granted does not include you; and, if you must know, it extends to the slaves, not to you, mistress of my soul, which adores you as if you were its Allah.

ZELINDA.

The clouds are gathering! The hour of my end is near! Clara, I know not what fears again foretell the end of our love, which will be a new example for lovers. I believed that the liberty that the Great Signor's generosity promised extended to us, but it was not so.

ZAIDA.

Hush—give no sign of your fears—you'll tell me later.

CADÍ.

Shall these three not enjoy your laudable mercy?

TURK.

Those two shall; but not this one, who offered to teach the elephant to speak elegant Turkish.

MADRIGAL.

By my mother's body! Is that where we are?

TURK.

Let him teach, and the time of his liberty shall come.

MADRIGAL [aside].

It won't be much of a time, if Andrea doesn't help. I'll run off, I'll fly.

CADÍ.

Catalina is so lovely that I cannot deny her her good fortune. Yet, while rejoicing, attend, my son, to fathering sons, and sow in more than one field.

TURK.

Catalina's a beautiful woman.

CADÍ.

And your desires range far.

TURK.

How can they range far, if they center on only one object?

CADÍ.

Time will tell.

TURK.

For all that, I'll follow your recommendation. Listen to me, Mamí.

MADRIGAL.

And listen, Master Cadí, to some things that concern you greatly.

CADÍ.

I'm listening, Madrigal.

MADRIGAL.

Then I'm speaking, and I say thus: let me have thirty escudos at once, to buy an elegant parrot being sold by an Indian. This peerless bird comes from the West Indies, to teach the foolish and the wise, the rich and the poor people of the world. I'll tell you what he says, since you already know that I know it by my high and holy science.

CADÍ.

I will give you the money; go to my house for it.

TURK.

Mamí, see that you do it, for I shall come back to it. Come, tinder of my fire, divine image of the blind god's mother. Come, you two, and enjoy the happy liberty I've granted you.

SECOND MUSICIAN.

May God grant you centuries of content!

MADRIGAL.

Disciple, where did you find such meager reward for the great good I did you? If you gave me life, you took my liberty. From this I infer, that there's no good without a catch, and no ill that doesn't hold some good—unless it's dying and eternal punishment.

[*Exeunt all but* MAMÍ *and* RUSTÁN, *who remain.*]

MAMÍ.

What do you think the Great Sultan wanted from me?

RUSTÁN.

I'm not certain, but I'd like to know.

MAMÍ.

As I thought, his fancy is fickle. He wants to rekindle his fire and return to the sweet blaze of his past pleasures: he asks to see his women right away. The Cadí's advice sat well with him; like a wise old man he told him: "Son, until you produce a son, I advise you to sow in many fields, for if not one then another will happily prove fertile."

RUSTÁN.

Based on that truth, Amurates errs but little. He offends the Sultana only slightly, for any affront is mitigated by the search for an heir.

MADRIGAL.

And actually it would be better not to have him from a Christian, out of all the captives he has. Who comes here?

RUSTÁN.

There are two of them.

MAMÍ.

These two will begin the procession.

RUSTÁN.

That's fitting, for they're extremely beautiful.

[*Enter* CLARA *and* LAMBERTO; *and, as has been stated,*
they are ZAIDA *and* ZELINDA.]

ZELINDA.

I can't recount my woes to you, for Rustán and Mamí are still here.

ZAIDA.

Keep them quiet, friend.

MAMÍ.

Each of you must pray that heaven grant you the good fortune to
have the Sultan look upon you with pleasure.

ZELINDA.

What is this? Does the Great Signor return to his habits?

RUSTÁN.

And now his captive women must promenade before him.

ZAIDA.

How is that? Did he so soon forget the singular beauty he adored?
His is not love, but lust.

RUSTÁN.

He seeks to sow an heir, in whoever it may be; that's the reason he
shows himself inconstant in love.

MAMÍ.

Where should I put Zelinda for his perusal? She seems fecund.
Would here in front work?

ZELINDA.

By no means! Zaida and Zelinda must be at the end of the fair line.

MAMÍ.

Let it be so, if that's your wish.

RUSTÁN.

Look, Zelinda: show the Great Signor your face; show him the lively,
manly sparkle of your two suns: perhaps he'll choose you, and you'll
be fortunate enough to give him the firstborn he desires. That will
be the end of the story. Stay here while I place the others in a long
line.

ZAIDA.

I obey.

ZELINDA.

And I thank you for placing us here.

[*Exit* MAMÍ *and* RUSTÁN.]

ZELINDA.

Now the saddest hour is surely come, lost before it even arrives! What will we do, my lady—I, a man, and you, pregnant? If Amurates notices your pretty face, he'll surely choose you; and no amount of prevention can remedy such clear misfortune. And if I were so unlucky that the Great Signor were to choose me . . .

ZAIDA.

I would look upon death if I saw you in such straits.

ZELINDA.

Should we not disfigure our faces?

ZAIDA.

That would force us to explain our misdeed, and any explanation would be useless, in that it would only condemn us.

ZELINDA.

Look what haste the renegade Mamí and that bad Christian Rustán make. Here come the captives; now they're all here; I'm sure if you count them you'll find more than two hundred.

ZAIDA.

And all of them, I'm sure, happy, with hopes very different from ours. Oh, how slowly the Great Signor passes by them all! He's viewed more than half.

ZELINDA.

Clara, an icy fear pierces my heart. May it please God to glue his feet to the earth before he reaches us!

ZAIDA.

Perhaps he'll decide before he gets here.

ZELINDA.

And if he reaches us, may he go blind!

[*Enter the* GRAND SIGNOR, MAMÍ, *and* RUSTÁN.]

TURK.

All those back there do not please me. Mamí, don't show me any more.

MAMÍ.

Well, one of these two will satisfy you.

RUSTÁN.

Look up, there's no room for shame here; raise your faces, you two.

TURK.

Catalina, there's no one to overcome me like you do! Yet, since the Cadí wants it, and it matters so much, bring me this one, Mamí.

[*The* TURK *throws a little handkerchief to* ZELINDA *and exits.*]

RUSTÁN.

You celebrate her good fortune with tears?

ZAIDA.

Yes; since I wanted to be the lucky one.

MAMÍ.

Let's go, Zelinda.

RUSTÁN.

We leave you alone and sad.

ZAIDA.

I'm jealous, and I'm a woman!

[*Exit* RUSTÁN *and* MAMÍ, *and they lead* ZELINDA,
who is LAMBERTO.]

Oh my sweet first love! Where are you headed? Who leads you to the strangest trial ever undergone by a true lover? This sad good-bye tells me that your excess will reveal my fault. What could help such confusion, Lamberto? You are a man, and they want you for a mother. Woe is me, I can see no remedy or excuse for the guilt of our just desire!

[*Enter the* SULTANA.]

SULTANA.

Zaida, what's wrong?

ZAIDA.

My lady, I don't know how to tell you of the pain in my soul:
Zelinda, my friend, who was with me just now, has been taken to the Great Signor.

SULTANA.

That worries you? Isn't she improving her fortune?

ZAIDA.

They're taking her to the grave; for she is a wretched man. We loved each other from our tender years, and we are both Transylvanian, from the same homeland and neighborhood. I was captured by misfortune— I won't tell you about it now, so as not to take time from thinking of some remedy for me. He found out with some certainty what my captivity had led to, which was to be brought to the seraglio, that sepulcher of my desires, and his own so pressed and vanquished him that he allowed himself to be captured by a clever scheme. He disguised himself as a woman, whose beauty instantly got her sold to the Turk without his owner knowing her. This strange plan achieved the aim of Alberto,[15] for this is the name of the wretch for whom I sorrow and perish. He knew me and I him, and from this knowledge I became pregnant, for so I am, and I am dying. Listen, fair Catalina, for I know that this name pleases you: What shall I do when such ills befall me? The unfortunate lad must be in the Turk's power already. That audacious lover, more constant than discreet! I can already hear Mamí saying, as he returns: "Zaida, we know the entire story of your love. Prepare to die, traitor, for the fire's lit for you, and the hook's ready for Lamberto!"[16]

SULTANA.

Come with me, fair Zaida, and have faith, for I hope, in God's great goodness, to get out of these straits.

[*Exeunt. Enter the* TURK, *who leads* LAMBERTO *by the neck, with an unsheathed dagger; the* CADÍ *and* MAMÍ *enter with him.*]

TURK.

It falls to me to put such vileness to death!

LAMBERTO.

Temper the haste that diminishes even your greatness; let me speak, and then give me whatever death you please.

---

15. Lamberto's name changes to the variant Alberto several times in this act.

16. This method of execution involved suspending the victim above sharpened hooks and forcing him to fall on them and agonize until finally expiring.

TURK.

Your lies won't stop me from spilling your blood.

CADÍ.

It is just to listen to the accused. Amurates, hear him out.

TURK.

Let him speak, and I shall listen.

MAMÍ [*aside*].

May he find an excuse.

LAMBERTO.

As a girl I heard a wise man describe the excellence and advantages that man has over woman; from that point on I wanted to be male, so I asked heaven for its help with this mercy. As a Christian woman it was denied to me, but not as a Moorish woman. Today I have begged Mohammed to grant me this novel mercy, moaning with tears and endearments, with fervent desires, with vows and promises, with prayers and sighs that would move a rock, all the way from the seraglio to here, silently and with great efficacy. Touched, the Prophet responded to my tender prayers and in an instant turned me from a woman into a strong man, and if such miracles deserve punishment, let the Prophet stand for me and for my innocence.

TURK.

Can this be, Cadí?

CADÍ.

And without a miracle, moreover.[17]

TURK.

I've never seen or heard of such a thing.

CADÍ.

I will tell you how this came to be whenever you please. I'd explain it now if the Sultana weren't coming, whom I see over there.

17. In the early modern imagination, there was no biological or real sex that distinguished the two genders; rather, gender was a fluid concept, and thoughts, actions, or the performance of any "manly" pursuits inappropriate to women (such as hunting, jumping, and the like) could turn a woman into a man; the same was considered true for men who engaged in "feminine" pursuits or associated with women in excess. See Laqueur 127.

TURK.

And she looks angry, it seems.

LAMBERTO.

There is hope in my hopelessness!

[*Enter the* SULTANA *and* ZAIDA.]

SULTANA.

How quickly and easily you've shown your lukewarm love through this trial! How soon your fancy leads you after the most immoderate desire! My lord, if you regret having raised me from my humble state to the peak of your majesty, then leave me, forget me. Afflicted as I am, I was truly afraid that these two would undo my happiness, that I would see this day and hour. But even in my pain I give thanks for this disenchantment, which puts an end to your toothsome and sweet deception, so that I do not perish. Cast them away from you, my lord, and from the seraglio this minute: for my love well deserves that you grant me this satisfaction and reassure my fears. All my pleasure depends on believing that you won't make another such mistake.

TURK.

I'd rather see you jealous than command the entire world, if it's true that jealousy is the offspring of Love, as they say. When it is not excessive, it feeds the flame of love, its glory and gladness.

SULTANA.

If you commit this and other outrages in order to produce heirs, I can assure you that I shall give them to you, and that they will be the first, for I have already missed three times the usual trouble that women get.

TURK.

O repository of prudence and beauty! With the news you've given me, I promise, by my faith as a well-born and well-bred Moor, to maintain that decorum toward you that you, my love, have maintained toward me. The heavens, in order to provide no further opportunity for the jealousy you've felt, have changed Zelinda into a man, as we have seen. He says so, and it's true, a fortunate miracle and a sign of his goodness.

SULTANA.

And it ensures our friendship without fear. Given such a miracle, marry Zaida to Zelinda, and, I tearfully beseech you, throw them out of the house straightaway; let them not remain a minute longer in your house, for I don't want to see things.

ZAIDA.

You've put me in a tight spot—I do not want to marry.

SULTANA.

You may come to bless me a thousand times for this. Grant them some favor, for I shall not see them again.

TURK.

Do it yourself, my lady.

RUSTÁN.

Has the world ever seen such a case?

TURK.

Dispose of these two as you will, my lady.

SULTANA.

Zelinda (or Zelindo) is now the Pasha of Chios.[18]

TURK.

How can your great power grant him so little, if it is mine? I make him the Pasha of Rhodes, and thus I satisfy his peerless valor.[19]

ALBERTO.

May the world vow obedience to you, and may heaven grant you the reward for your pious nature, o rose placed among thorns to the glory of all roses!

TURK.

You don't just move me, you force me to perform magnificent deeds! To celebrate the certain prophecies you've given me of your delivery, I want the Cadí to make the nights into days; let endless luminaries be placed in the windows, and with wondrous spectacles may my vassals set themselves to extraordinary celebrations. Let the holy

18. Chios is an island situated in the Aegean Sea off the coast of Greece. It was an important post, as it contributed much to the Ottoman treasury.

19. For a discussion of this episode, see Fuchs 2003, 83–86.

and profane great games of Rome be restored, and the Greek ones as well, and any other excellent ones there may be.

CADÍ.

Your will shall be done, and may this great hope come true. And may you, with honest use, be as fecund as Rachel.[20]

SULTANA.

You two get going right away, for I'm determined never to see you again, so as not to witness another occasion that might lead to folly.

ALBERTO.

As soon as I have my letters, I'll be out of your fair sight, my lady, and shall always remember your wit and courtesy.

ZAIDA.

And I, fair Catalina, shall hold your discretion peerless and divine.

TURK.

These are proper praises for her marvelous goodness. Come, beloved Christian, for I want to give you once more my soul as your spoils.

SULTANA.

Thus I carry off the prize for these vexations; for when quarreling lovers make peace, they please and satisfy the senses, which are undone with anger.

[*Exeunt omnes. Enter* MADRIGAL *and* ANDREA.]

MADRIGAL.

Here they are, Andrea, and I shall be most fortunate if you bring me to safety, since there's no reason to wait out the ten years of my elephantine professorship; it's better to run from good men than to ask them for help.

ANDREA.

Isn't that clear?

MADRIGAL.

The thirty escudos in gold are the price of a unique Indian parrot, which lacks nothing but speech.

ANDREA.

If it's mute, you praise it well.

---

20. This may be a reference to Jacob's wife Rachel, mother to Joseph and Benjamin in the book of Genesis. Rachel is not typically invoked as a model of fecundity.

MADRIGAL.

That ignorant Cadí . . . !

ANDREA.

What about the Cadí?

MADRIGAL.

I'll tell you wonders along the way. Come, I'm dying to be in Madrid already, with people forming circles around me to ask. "How is that? Tell us, captive, on your life. Is it true that the Sultana who rules today in Turkey is named Catalina, and that she is a Christian, with a *don* before her name, and that de Oviedo is her surname?" Oh, what things I'll tell them! And I even plan—since I'm already half there, being a poet—to become a playwright and compose the history of this girl without straying one jot from the truth, playing the same character there that I do here. Isn't it something, Andrea, to see the groundlings[21] so astonished, swallowing flies and even wasps unawares just to see me? But they'll take their revenge, perhaps, by calling me names that vex and bother me. Farewell, famous Constantinople! Pera and Permas, farewell! Farewell, Chifutí and even Guedí stairs! Farewell, fair garden of Visitax! Farewell, great temple of St. Sophia, though you now serve as a great mosque! Shipyards, farewell, and may the devil take you, for each day you place in the water a galley fully built, from the keel to the crow's nest, ready to set sail![22]

ANDREA.

It's time to go, Madrigal.

MADRIGAL.

I know, and there are just three hundred more things to which I must bid my usual sweet farewell.

ANDREA.

Let's go, for so many farewells are nonsense.

21. As at Shakespeare's Globe, groundlings were those with the most inexpensive tickets, who stood at ground level in Spanish *corrales*, open-air theaters often set up in patios of larger houses and later housed in dedicated buildings.

22. Cervantes refers to actual places in Constantinople. Note the emphasis on the amazing rate at which the Sultan's navy grows.

[*Exeunt. Enter* SALEC, *the renegade, and* ROBERTO
(*the two who began the play*).]

SALEC.

That's her, no doubt, according to what I was told by Rustán, the
eunuch who is my friend.

ROBERTO.

I don't doubt it; for that miraculous transformation into a man was
the wise Lamberto's scheme.

SALEC.

Let us head to the Great Court, for he may already be leaving with
the title of Great Pasha of Rhodes, which they say the Great Signor
has given him.

ROBERTO.

May God grant it! Oh if only I could see them first, before death
closes these eyes of mine!

SALEC.

Let's go, and may heaven ease your pains.

[*Exeunt. Shawms sound; they begin to place luminaries; enter the*
GARZONS *of the* TURK *on the stage, running with lighted torches,
crying out: "Long live the Great Sultana Doña Catalina de Oviedo!
May she deliver happily!" Then* RUSTÁN *and* MAMÍ *enter and tell the*
GARZONS.]

RUSTÁN.

Raise your voices, lads; may the Great Sultana Doña Catalina be
praised—the Great Sultana and a Christian, glory and honor of her
tender and Christian years, honor of her nation and homeland! May
God make her desires so just and holy that a new and true history
may be written of her liberty and memory.

[*The shawms and voices of the* GARZONS *sound again. Curtain.*]

       ⊠   FINIS. ⊠

In recent years, there has been a veritable explosion of monographs and collections on the early modern Mediterranean, on travel literature, and on the relations between Europe and the Muslim world. There has also been some attempt to edit or reedit primary texts on these topics, as in the case of Daniel Vitkus's *Three Turk Plays*, which includes *Selimus, Emperor of the Turks* (1594), *A Christian Turned Turk* (1612), and *The Renegado* (1623). In the field of Cervantes studies, there has been renewed attention to the representation of North Africa and of Muslim or Morisco subjects, both in María Antonia Garcés's *Cervantes in Algiers*, awarded the MLA James Russell Lowell Prize for Best Book in 2003, and in Barbara Fuchs's *Passing for Spain: Cervantes and the Fictions of Identity*.

PRIMARY SOURCES

Anonymous. 2000. *Viaje de Turquía*. Ed. Fernando García Salinero. Madrid: Cátedra.

Cervantes Saavedra, Miguel de. 1870. *The Voyage to Parnassus; Numantia, A Tragedy; The Commerce of Algiers*. Trans. Gordon Willoughby James Gyll. London: Alex. Murray & Son.

———. 1937. *The first part of the delightful history of the most ingenious knight Don Quixote of the Mancha*. Trans. Thomas Shelton. Harvard Classics, vol. 14. New York: P. F. Collier & Son.

———. 1969. *Los trabajos de Persiles y Sigismunda*. Ed. Juan Bautista Avalle-Arce. Madrid: Castalia.

———. 1992. *Los baños de Argel ; Pedro de Urdemalas*. Ed. Jean Canavaggio. Madrid: Taurus.

———. 1995. *Obra completa*. Ed. Florencio Sevilla Arroyo and Antonio Rey Hazas. 3 vols. Alcalá de Henares: Alianza / Centro de Estudios Cervantinos.

———. 1996. *Eight Interludes*. Trans. Dawn Smith. London: Everyman.

————. 1998. *Obra completa*. Ed. Florencio Sevilla Arroyo and Antonio Rey Hazas. 21 vols. Madrid: Alianza.

————. 1999. *Don Quixote*. Trans. Burton Raffel. Ed. Diana de Armas Wilson. New York: Norton.

————. 2001. *Novelas ejemplares*. Ed. Harry Sieber. 2 vols. Madrid: Cátedra.

————. 2005. *Don Quixote*. Trans. Edith Grossman. New York: Ecco.

Covarrubias Orozco, Sebastián de. 1998. *Tesoro de la lengua castellana o española* (1611). Ed. Martín de Riquer. Barcelona: Alta Fulla.

Delicado, Francisco. 2000. *La Lozana Andaluza*. Ed. Claude Allaigre. Madrid: Cátedra.

Diccionario de Autoridades. 1979. Ed. Real Academia Española. 3 vols. Madrid: Gredos.

Haedo, Diego de. 1927. *Topografía e historia de Argel*. 3 vols. Madrid: Sociedad de Bibliófilos Españoles.

SECONDARY SOURCES

Anderson, Ellen M. 1993. "Playing at Moslem and Christian: Construction of Gender and the Representation of Faith in Cervantes' Captivity Plays." *Cervantes* 13, no. 2:37–59.

Andrews, Walter G., and Mehmet Kalpakli. 2005. *The Age of Beloveds: Love and the Beloved in Early-Modern Ottoman and European Culture and Society*. Durham: Duke University Press.

Barbour, Richard. 2003. *Before Orientalism: London's Theatre of the East, 1576–1626*. Cambridge: Cambridge University Press.

Bartels, Emily. 1993. *Spectacles of Strangeness: Imperialism, Alienation, and Marlowe*. Philadelphia: University of Pennsylvania Press.

Benassar, Bartolomé, and Lucille Benassar. 1989. *Los cristianos de Alá: la fascinante aventura de los renegados*. Trans. José Luis Gil Aristu. Madrid: NEREA.

Boon, Jessica. 2007. "The Agony of the Virgin: The Swoons and Crucifixion of Mary in Sixteenth-Century Castilian Passion Treatises." *Sixteenth-Century Journal* 38, no. 1:3–26.

Braudel, Fernand. 1972. *The Mediterranean and the Mediterranean World in the Age of Philip II*. Trans. Siân Reynolds. 2 vols. New York: Harper & Row.

Canavaggio, Jean. 1990. *Cervantes*. Trans. J. R. Jones. New York: Norton.

Chew, Samuel. 1937. *The Crescent and the Rose: Islam and England during the Renaissance*. New York: Oxford University Press.

Elliott, J. H. 1963. *The Revolt of the Catalans: A Study in the Decline of Spain*. Cambridge: Cambridge University Press, 1963.

————. 2002. *Imperial Spain 1469–1716*. London: Penguin.

El-Rouayheb, Khaled. *Before Homosexuality in the Arab-Islamic World, 1500–1800*. Chicago: University of Chicago Press, 2005.

Farrés, Gil. 1959. *Historia de la moneda española*. Madrid: Diana.

Friedman, Ellen. 1983. *Spanish Captives in North Africa in the Early Modern Age*. Madison: University of Wisconsin Press.

Fuchs, Barbara. 2001. *Mimesis and Empire: The New World, Islam, and European Identities*. Cambridge: Cambridge University Press.

————. 2003. *Passing for Spain: Cervantes and the Fictions of Identity*. Urbana: University of Illinois Press.

Garcés, Maria Antonia. 2002. *Cervantes in Algiers: A Captive's Tale*. Nashville: Vanderbilt University Press.

Hess, Andrew C. 1978. *The Forgotten Frontier: A History of the Sixteenth-Century Ibero-African Frontier*. Chicago: University of Chicago Press.

Imber, Colin. 1997. "Women, Marriage and Property." In Zilfi, ed., 81–104.

Irigoyen García, Javier. 2005. "Moriscos conversos en Berbería: La heterotopía de *Los baños de Argel*." In *Actas del Congreso "El Siglo de Oro en el Nuevo Milenio,"* ed. Carlos Mata Induráin and Miguel Zugasti, 2:911–17. Pamplona: Universidad de Navarra.

Johnson, Carroll B. 2000. *Cervantes and the Material World*. Urbana: University of Illinois Press, 2000.

La Du, Robert R. 1960. "Lazarillo's Stepfather Is Hanged . . . Again." *Hispania* 43, no. 2 (May): 243–44.

Laqueur, Thomas. 1990. *Making Sex: Body and Gender from the Greeks to Freud*. Cambridge, Mass.: Harvard University Press, 1990.

Longino, Michele. 2002. *Orientalism in French Classical Drama*. Cambridge: Cambridge University Press.

Mariscal, George. 1994. "*La Gran Sultana* and the Issue of Cervantes' Modernity." *Revista de estudios hispánicos* 28, no. 2:185–211.

Martínez López, Enrique. 2003. "Rebuznos de casta en un menú cervantino sobre los que con desazón comen 'duelos y quebrantos los sábados' y los motejados de 'cazoleros' o 'berenjeneros.'" In *En gustos se comen géneros: Congreso internacional comida y literatura*, 3 vols., ed. Sara Poot Herrera, 3:107–33. Mérida: Instituto de cultura de Yucatán.

Mas, Albert. 1967. *Les Turcs dans la Littérature Espagnole du Siècle d'Or*. 2 vols. Paris: Centre des Recherches Hispaniques.

Matar, Nabil. 1998. *Islam in Britain, 1558–1685*. Cambridge: Cambridge University Press.

———. 1999. *Turks, Moors and Englishmen in the Age of Discovery*. New York: Columbia University Press.

———, ed. 2003. *In the Lands of the Christians: Arabic Travel Writing in the Seventeenth Century*. New York: Routledge.

McKendrick, Melveena. 2002. "Works for the Stage." *The Cambridge Companion to Cervantes*. Ed. Anthony J. Cascardi. Cambridge: Cambridge University Press.

Pedani-Fabris, Maria Pia. 1997. "Veneziani a Costantinopoli all fine del XVI Secolo." *Quaderni di Studi Arabi*, supplement to vol. 15, *Veneziani in Levante, Musulmani a Venezia*, 67–84.

Sevilla Arroyo, Florencio, and Antonio Rey Hazas. 1998. "Introducción: El teatro de Cervantes: Primera época." *El trato de Argel*, in Cervantes 1998, 2: i–xl.

Shaw, Stanford J. 1991. *The Jews of the Ottoman Empire and the Turkish Republic*. New York: New York University Press.

Singh, Jyotsna, and Ivo Kamps, eds. 2001. *Travel Knowledge: European "Discoveries" in the Early Modern Period*. New York: Palgrave Macmillan.

Vitkus, Daniel. 2001. *Piracy, Slavery, and Redemption. Barbary Captivity Narratives from Early Modern England*. New York: Columbia University Press.

———. 2003. *Turning Turk: English Theater and the Multicultural Mediterranean, 1570–1630*. New York: Palgrave Macmillan.

———, ed. *Three Turk Plays from Early Modern England: Selimus, A Christian Turned Turk, and The Renegado*. New York: Columbia University Press, 2000.

Wilson, Diana de Armas. 2000. *Cervantes, the Novel and the New World*. Oxford: Oxford University Press.

Zilfi, Madeline. 1997. "'We Don't Get Along': Women and *Hul* Divorce in the Eighteenth Century." In Zilfi ed., 264–96.

———, ed. 1997. *Women in the Ottoman Empire: Middle Eastern Women in the Early Modern Era.* Leiden: Brill.

Acknowledgments

These translations were made possible by a Collaborative Research Grant from the National Endowment for the Humanities, for which we are very grateful. We would also like to thank Nabil Matar, who provided the inspiration for this project, and the friends and colleagues in various fields who graciously contributed their expertise: Palmira Brummett, María Judith Feliciano, María Antonia Garcés, Javier Irigoyen-García, E. Ann Matter, J Melvin, Ben Nathans, Leslie Pierce, Larry Silver, and Michael Solomon.